CONTENTS

The Worth of Nations

The Boston, Melbourne, Oxford Conversazioni
on Culture and Society

The Worth of Nations

Bernard Levin

Simon Schama

Donald S. Carne-Ross

Hugh Trevor-Roper

Ben Whitaker

Liah Greenfeld

Peter M. Oppenheimer

Kenneth R. Minogue

Roger Scruton

Edited by Claudio Véliz

Introduction by Jon Westling

BOSTON UNIVERSITY

THE UNIVERSITY PROFESSORS

Boston University, Boston 02215
© 1993 by the Trustees of Boston University
All rights reserved. Published 1993
Printed in the United States of America

Library of Congress Cataloging-in-Publication Data

Boston, Melbourne, Oxford Conversazioni on Culture and Society (4th :
     1992 : Boston University)
        The worth of nations : the Boston, Melbourne, Oxford Conversazioni
    on Culture and Society / Bernard Levin . . . [et al.] ; edited by
    Claudio Véliz.
             p.   cm.
        Includes bibliographical references.
        ISBN 0-87270-103-4 (alk. paper)
        1. Nationalism.   I. Levin, Bernard.   II. Véliz, Claudio.
    III. Title.
    JC311.B663   1992
    320.5′4 — dc20   93-17354
                                                                         CIP

The opinions expressed in this publication, and in all other publications issued
under the auspices of *The Boston, Melbourne, Oxford Conversazioni on Culture and
Society, The Boston Conversazioni,* or The University Professors of Boston University, are the responsibility solely of the authors.

Introduction

AUGUSTUS, as part of his vast urban renewal of Rome, built a portico called *Ad Nationes,* in which "the images of all known nations were set up." Unfortunately, our sources do not tell us how many images the portico contained, or what they looked like, but the very existence of such a monument is worthy of note. It suggests that even two millennia ago the idea that the world was a world of nations was in the air.

In the modern world, the nation is an idea whose time has not only come but endured. Unlike some once-fashionable organizing principles — mercantilism and communism, for example — neither the nation nor nationalism shows any signs of superannuation. It has indeed become a truism of every editorial page with any pretensions to intellectual weightiness that the end of the Cold War has revealed a florid growth of national enthusiasms — and national enmities — that totalitarianism had obscured but not eradicated.

Thus the fourth in the continuing series of Boston, Melbourne, Oxford Conversazioni on Culture and Society, which was held at Boston University on November 12, 13, and 14, 1992, provided an opportune occasion for reflection on the nation and on nationalism. The essays in this volume, which are the results of that reflection, are evidence of the pervasiveness and complexity of the subject.

Books of collected essays, proceedings of conferences and the like, are frequently prefaced by apologies for the heterogeneity of the contributions. No such apology is needed here. The nation has become so central a fact in all our lives, and its political, social, intellectual, emotional, and cultural ramifications are so immense, that an attempt to impose neat categories on the sprawling reality, or to pretend to an intellectual tidiness that does not and perhaps cannot exist, would diminish the importance of the volume.

Instead, the contributors have provided us with a series of exploratory tunnels into the central massif of the nation. Their knowledge of history, economics, literary criticism, sociology, philosophy, journalism, politics (both theoretical and applied), business, and law has been brought to bear on the crucial questions of the origin, the changing nature and the fate, insofar as it can be discerned, of nation, nationality and nationalism.

At any time, the opportunity to learn from such a distinguished group of scholars and thinkers would be welcome. At this moment in history, the opportunity to learn from them about a topic of such consequence for all of us is an occasion for gratitude to Professor Claudio Véliz and the other organizers of the Boston, Melbourne, Oxford Conversazioni.

For many reasons, this book does not seek to surround the essays with the debate and discussion that they provoked when they were delivered. But with their publication the conversation that was begun in Boston can now extend to others who seek "the truth whereby the nations live."

JON WESTLING
Executive Vice President and Provost
Boston University

The Worth of Nations

"Thou Hast Multiplied the Nation, and Not Increased the Joy" — Isaiah 9.3

BERNARD LEVIN

I N HENRY THE FIFTH, act three, in a pause in the battle for Harfleur, Shakespeare brings together an Englishman, a Scotsman, a Welshman, and an Irishman; not, as you may think, to start one of those jokes which begin with just such a cast, but as far as one can tell, simply to set them quarreling. It is the Welshman, Fluellen, who starts the trouble (the Welsh have not stopped yet, four hundred years on), by baiting the Irishman, Captain Macmorris. Fluellen is clearly out to suggest that the Irish regiments were thin on the ground when he says, "Captain Macmorris, I think, look you, under your correction, there is not many of your nation — " but he is instantly interrupted, and the very word triggers off the explosion in Macmorris, who goes berserk, shouting, "Of my nation? What is my nation? Is a villain, and a bastard, and a knave, and a rascal? What is my nation? Who talks of my nation?"

Fortunately, the bugle sounds to call them away, before they can come to blows, though not before Macmorris has threatened to cut Fluellen's head off. But this tiny vignette — and remember that by then Shakespeare did nothing by accident — encapsulates the paradox that puzzled Captain Macmorris as it puzzles us: We do not really understand what a nation is, but we are ready to fight for it.

Coming from Britain as I do, I have recently been experiencing an astonishingly vivid and powerful demonstration of the paradox. In 1975, Britain had a referendum on the question: Should we remain in what was then called the Common Market? The turnout was huge, closely comparable to that of a General Election, but because there was only a Yes/No vote, the ballots were counted not by constituencies but in one huge tally in what was then the largest indoor arena in the country. (A touching memory comes to the surface; I recall that for ease of moving the huge bundles of votes, those in charge of the count had requisitioned three thousand supermarket trolleys.)

1

At the press conference the day before the vote, someone asked the head scrutineer what he would do if Yes and No votes were so close that a recount was demanded. He gritted his teeth and said, "We'll have one." It was not necessary. Among the twenty-six million who voted in General Election numbers, almost 70 percent had said Yes. Had the British at last agreed with John Donne that

> No man is an island, entire of itself; every man is a piece of the continent, a
> part of the main; if a clod be washed away by the sea, Europe is the less, as
> well as if a promontory were . . . ?

I do not believe it. A Common Market posed no threat; for most people a market is a friendly thing, and indeed outside the cities the weekly "market day" was and is at the very heart of rural Britain. Let Napoleon call us "a nation of shopkeepers"; we accept the charge and proclaim ourselves proud of it, and anyway we beat Napoleon, so he's a fine one to talk.

So far, we have not had a referendum on the European Community, and with every day that passes it becomes more obvious that the reason we are denied a straightforward choice is that the 70-30 figure of 1975 is all too likely to be 30-70 today.

But why? Those who argue the cause speak of restrictions on our social policies, of compulsory new methods of raising and slaughtering cattle, of interference with long-held fishing rights, of the danger from criminals with the abolition of border controls, even of the ruin of the purveyors of duty-free goods. None of these well-argued reasons for caution over British membership of the EC has even the slightest interest for the public in general, who neither know nor care anything about any of these possible problems. For millions upon millions in Britain the only fear from the EC is the fear that Britain will no longer *be* Britain, but a province of Europe, and moreover, only one province among many.

Now when any dispassionate observer, whether from Britain or from outside, is apprised of this feeling, the first response must inevitably be incredulity. For decades there have been serious, powerful, and relentless organizations in Scotland and Wales, the members of which, with ever-increasing stridency, have demanded *not* to be part of Britain, but of — well, it is not very clear of what. If Britain is to be lopped of her Scottish and Welsh provinces — while, incidentally, the great majority in her Northern Ireland extremity demand to be even closer to the Mother Country — what will be left to keep the Union Jack flying? (Though in any case it will not be the Union Jack; the departing provinces would take their parts of the national flag with them, as disgruntled children who are losing the game take their ball home.)

But that, surely, is the point. There is no place on earth, I guess, too small to be made even smaller. The independent nation called Andorra, which nestles high in the Pyrenees, straddling the French-Spanish border, holds 14,000 citizens in nine villages. There is an even mightier nation, San Marino, which can boast a population something over 19,000, in a mere crack in the Italian Alps. But I will wager that both of them have organizations — peaceful ones, I trust — which demand independence for one tiny corner of their tiny worlds. And for that matter — turning from the microcosm to the macrocosm — who has not seen in this country a bumper sticker reading "Keep your Confederate money — the South will rise again." A joke, of course; but the Civil War wasn't.

Let me return for a moment to Britain and her attitude to the European Community. Britain is notorious for insularity, though in truth France has far more, and she adds unsociability to it, which we British certainly don't. But I have often wondered what the British would be like if, in some prehistoric seabed upheaval, the English Channel had been filled in. You will, of course, have noticed what I called it, which is what it is indeed always called in Britain, while the literal French are content to call it what it looks like, La Manche, a sleeve. But is it true, I ask, that the mere existence of the Channel makes us suspicious of those who live beyond it?

A moment's thought must make it clear that that cannot be the answer. Countless quarrels and wars have scarred Europe without the British having anything to do with them; the lights have gone out without us touching the switch. But then, another question, and a more significant one, rears its head: Do we British have a concept of nationhood that is different from that of other countries? Well, the word "chauvinism" has entered the English language, but it certainly didn't originate there. Our patriotism is strong, but it is exceptionally unobtrusive; indeed a jingo attitude will almost invariably provoke embarrassment. There is a short story by Kipling — and nobody will deny that he wore his patriotism on his sleeve — in which a boastful school visitor, waving the flag, attracts nothing but revulsion in the boys he thinks he is inspiring.

Still, reticence in such matters can hardly be more than a clue; the real trouble is that we lack clues to the nature of nationhood itself, for until we have understood it we cannot appraise its worth. I find it amazing that there are many people in Britain — and I think in the United States also, but nowhere else — who have an attitude of indifference, or even downright hostility, to the idea of a people bound by a common thread, and in every other way indistinguishable; that is, who neither feel nor wish to feel a sense of nationhood. Nor is this attitude confined to the ignorant or indifferent; for me, at least, it passes belief to hear Sir Edward Heath, who has been Prime Minister of Britain, gaily conceding that his idea of community is a united states of Europe. And not long ago I heard one of the most successful writers of children's books, who sells hundreds of thousands of copies, giving an extended interview on BBC radio, in which again and again she said "Britain," in a context which would have naturally led most of us to say "we." Listening to it was a startling demonstration, however unconscious, of a wish not to be part of what, after all, she *is* part, even if only by formal nationality.

It is, of course, easy to forget that no one at birth requests a particular nationality; perhaps we should institute a system by which when any young man or woman comes of age, he or she should be given a choice of nationality, having previously been in a kind of limbo with no nationality at all. There could be ceremonies akin to a coming-of-age or for that matter a confirmation or a Bar Mitzvah, but why stop there? Officials from different countries would attend these festivities and examine the most recent batch for future character and loyalty, while the shrewder and more commercially minded young people would auction themselves to the highest bidder.

But those absurdities conceal a puzzling reality. Why do we almost always automatically accept the nationality of our birth? Of course, habit is powerful; by the time young people do come of age, they have been imbued with their own nation's customs, comradeship, quality, opportunities, and, above all, language. Yet even rebellious youth, much given to stamping out of the family home, does not think in terms of comparison with other nationalities; even when visits to other countries — particularly the close-packed nations of western Europe — have resulted in rhapsodies for the countries visited, and an expressed wish to live there — even, indeed, if the wish is carried out, the thought of changing nationality is manifestly felt as nothing less than bizarre.

It is a truism that, in countries which are at least reasonably free and reasonably prosperous, and even in many countries that have neither of those benefits, we find the inhabitants not only content to be, say, Ruritanians, but no less content to declare that Ruritania is truly the best country in the world.

Take me, though I do not claim that I am the very pattern and exemplar of British nationality. I like the absence of class in America and most of Europe; I like pleasant routines such as the Spanish siesta; I like the French attitude to food — that it is to enjoy, not to measure cholesterol counts; I like the relaxed Italian habit of ignoring time. All these, when I measure them against the customs of my own country, seem to have the advantage. But it never crosses my mind to throw in my lot permanently with any of them.

It is very unlikely that even the most foolhardy investigator would try to make a table of excellence in nations, with the best at the top and the worst at the bottom, and the ones at the top preening themselves, while the ones at the bottom are forever crying, "We wuz robbed!" Yet I tell you that the impossible has been achieved; just such a table exists, and exists moreover in a form which is almost impossible to impugn or even question. Many of you must know the book; it is called *The World Human Rights Guide,* and is now published in its third edition by the Oxford University Press. It was created single-handedly in the fertile mind of Charles Humana, who, I regret to record, died a few months ago, just as the most recent edition was going to press.

For those who are not familiar with the book, please allow me to say something about it, because it is very close to the heart not only of human rights, but of the nature and meaning of nation and nationalism.

With astonishing ingenuity, Charles Humana drew up a taxonomy of rights; forty questions are listed for every country, and the questions are divided into "Freedom to," "Freedom from," "Freedom for or rights to," "Legal rights," and "Personal rights." The questions range from "Can citizens freely travel outside their country?" to "Is there political censorship of the press?" and "Is there a right to practice homosexuality between consenting adults?" to "Is there a right to practice any religion or none?" In addition, each country is rated for type of rule, life expectancy, income per head, and infant mortality; when all the data are collected, they are weighted against 100 percent. You may be interested to learn that the near-best scorers — Sweden, Denmark, and the Netherlands — score 98 percent, Norway 97, and Britain 94. Of the worst, China and Libya score 23 percent, Iraq 19, North Korea 17, and Ethiopia 13. But Finland scores 99.

This, of course, is only one aspect of life in a nation, but it is surely a very significant one. It is a pity that we cannot take opinion polls in Ethiopia, Iraq, North Korea, and Libya, asking a random selection of the nationals of the world's worst tyrannies whether they feel proud of their nation, but I have an uneasy feeling that many of them would say Yes, and not just because a member of the secret police was within earshot.

As it happens, there may shortly be a good deal of evidence on the subject. Who would have thought that the era of the great migrations, which finished many centuries ago, may be coming back? Already, the settled nations are finding themselves, however naturally well disposed to refugees ("Give me . . . your huddled masses"), compelled to shut more and more doors, as the ending of the Soviet Empire, together with the apparently inexorable decline in the standard of living of the poorest of the world, drives many thousands — it will be millions very soon — to find a world elsewhere.

We see it in the flood of refugees from the former eastern empire; we see it more intensely than ever on the American-Mexican border; we see it in North Africa, when every night now, little boats set off for the winking lighthouses of Spain — for them a country as golden as El Dorado, compared to their African life. What does nationhood mean to these people?

What does it mean to a family with no bread? What does it mean to men and women who see their neighbors slip away towards, they think, a life not bordered by privation?

The other end of the scale offers an astonishing contrast. The collapse of communism could be predicted; I had been predicting it for more than twenty years. What was almost equally obvious was that the Soviet Union, when it died, would leave a legacy of fragments, each claiming nationhood, and willing — indeed eager — to fight for it. Seventy years of cramming nationalism into the communist shirt of Nessus had done nothing but intensify every limb of every would-be free republic; and when the burning shirt was flung off, not only was there an instant multiplication of self-governing satrapies, but within that multiplication there were those who were not content with nationhood, but would not rest until they had fought to the death in the making of their own miniature empire.

But there was much more to come from the cave of nationalism. Every day now, greater horrors are reported from the internecine slaughter in what was once, for good or ill, Yugoslavia. Again, just as the Soviet Empire denied the very idea of a nation, unless it was the artificial, if not meaningless, Soviet version, so did Tito believe (or, more likely, pretend to believe) that this grotesque spatchcock monster was a nation, when to everyone's surprise it turned out to be several nations, each hating all the others in the name of nation. Had nobody read the history of the ending of the First World War and the ludicrous peace that followed it? Did nobody think, when Hitler demanded his rights, saying that they had been stolen from Germany and were now to be restored, that one day similar rights would be demanded elsewhere?

And now even Czechoslovakia, another hybrid, insists on being a Czecho and a Slovakia, where much care and good luck will be required to stop them fighting too. Any night now, I shall be dreaming that the European Community had embarked upon a bloodletting more savage than that in Yugoslavia, where position papers, reports, guidance documents, first and second drafts, are being hurled at innocent women and children, whose cries rend heaven but are not heeded, because the combatants have sworn, in the name of their nations, never to sheathe the file until every enemy has been extirpated in a merciless rain of *aide-mémoire*, annotations, proposals, faxes, shorthand-notebooks, and statements of policy, if any. Wordsworth, of all people, chips in here:

Two Voices are there: one is of the sea,
One of the mountains; each a mighty Voice.

It is not, I think, too fanciful to think of the two voices as the two irreconcilable natures of nationhood; indeed Wordsworth helps us, because that

---

sonnet was written in mourning for the subjugation of Switzerland. On the one hand, the call of nation binds a people, not just in fraternity, but — again and again throughout history — to noble and selfless endeavors. How many millions have gone to their deaths proudly and with no regret, when the bugle has sounded and the cry of "the nation in danger" was heard? And how many other millions have died to destroy an enemy with a different name to its nation? Beneath the name of nation, the greatest good and the greatest evil have cohabited, and there is no way of disentangling the one from the other. It was in the very making of a nation that Cavour said, "If we did for ourselves the things we do for Italy, what scoundrels we should be."

The flood has not yet petered out, and shows no sign of doing so. Every time we try to count the number of nations on this earth, we find more of them; some have split off from a motherland, some have invented themselves, some have turned to partition when it was clear that two factions would never agree. When I last counted the nations of the world, the tally was over 160, and it is certainly greater now.

At least once or twice a month a bomb goes off in central London. The men who put the bombs there have long since forgotten why they are doing it; to kill, injure, or at least discommode the people of the capital is an end in itself. But once they had a goal; it was to make two nations one. Decades have passed, and many dead have been buried, and still the claim is pressed, and pressed, all too often, by bomb and gun. The irony of the story is the fact that in the nation that is supposed to yearn for her lost sons and daughters, only a handful care one way or the other.

Yet the day when nations cease to quarrel has not yet come, and there is no sign of it on the horizon. There is a clue in the Psalms; the passage runs, "Put them in fear, O Lord: that the nations may know themselves to be but men." How many tragedies have been played out because the nations thought themselves more than men! And yet, throughout history, great and wonderful deeds have been done just because the nations thought themselves more than men. The pendulum is irregular, but it swings.

Perhaps I should conclude with what must certainly have a claim on the title of the most optimistic statement about nations ever made. It is to be found in London, at the headquarters of the BBC. When the building was being erected, in 1927, one of the governors of the then-infant organization, Dr. John Rendall, was set the task of creating a motto for it. After much cogitation he came up with an answer, which was accepted by the Board; there is no remaining evidence as to whether it was immediately accepted or whether it was adopted only after much heated debate. At any rate, it was adopted, and if you go to Broadcasting House and look inside the entrance hall, you will see the proud claim, running round the ceiling, picked out in gold lettering, and it says: "Nation shall speak peace unto nation." One day, let us hope that that brave, bold, brazen, barefaced, beautiful wish will come true.

Woodland, Homeland, Fatherland: Thoughts on the Ecology of Nationalism

SIMON SCHAMA

T HERE ARE COUNTLESS national parks in Europe but there is only one true wildwood: an authentically primeval forest that has never been cut, cleared, or replanted. Its site is Bialowieza, by the village of the White Tower, about thirty miles northeast of Bialystok. Today, the frontier between Poland and Belorussia cuts right through the forest. But for centuries it lay deep in ancestral Lithuania, not the Baltic republic but the Polish Lithuania celebrated and invoked in the poetry of Mickiewicz and Milosz and in the eerie, haunted prose of Tadeusz Konwicki. Get up in the mists of a springtime dawn and you can still wander alone in a startling undisturbed ecology: a great vegetable ossuary where prone carcasses of dead hornbeams and spindle trees lie gently rotting in deep and scummy peat bogs; where others lean at crazy angles supported by the vast trunks of centenarian oaks.

There is wild garlic and wild honey in these scented woods; countless varieties of fungus spreading riotously amidst the woodmold; beaver lodges piled up beside alder trees standing next to black water. If you are very lucky and very quiet you might get a glimpse of elk or lynx or even the Lithuanian bison, the *zubr,* on its way to feed off the fragrant *Hierochloe odorata,* the meadowgrass that grows in the spaces opened by the death of ancient trees.

The biodiversity of the *puszcza Bialowieza* proclaims its great antiquity, its miraculous escape from the scientific forestry of the Enlightenment and the nineteenth century, with their obsession with taxonomically ordered plantations, graduated by age and species into uniform blocks of trees, accessible for serial harvesting. From at least the fifteenth century Bialowieza was recognized as a habitat uniquely packed with species — like the bison, described in ancient geographies like those of Pliny and Strabo, but which had become extinct elsewhere. And this sense of the place as a living biological *Wunderkammer* made it passionately coveted as the most extraordinary hunting ground between the Urals and the Atlantic. Paradoxically, it has been the persistence of the most ancient pastime of death into the age of the nation-state that has guaranteed the survival of the forest.

But it has also made Bialowieza a place bitterly and brutally contested between warring cultures, each of which associates the antiquity of the woodland with its own national legitimacy. For there are graves in this woodland: Polish, German, Russian, Jewish, some marked, many more unmarked. For the Poles in particular, the immemorial longevity of the forests serves as a correlate of their own sense of tragic imperishability. But we are not just talking poetic metaphors here, powerful though they are in the construction of national memory and identity. For each time that the Polish *state* collapsed or was devoured alive by predatory neighbors (thrice in the eighteenth century); each time its patriotic warriors made attempts to resurrect it (twice in the nineteenth century, twice more in the twentieth); it was the forest, *this* forest, and others to the north and south, that provided shelter, camouflage, and graveyard for the partisans.

Artur Grottger's series of lithographs from the 1860s, like Adam Mickiewicz's *Pan Tadeusz,* identify the forest depths, the "commonwealth of bison and bear," as a place of freedom and death; of consummation and rebirth; the Calvary of what, paradoxically, the greatest Polish poets have always celebrated as "Lithuania." But it is precisely because the Poles do *not* have a monopoly on the national mystique of the *Ur-wald* that the border woodlands have seen so much trouble. Even the European culture which of necessity was least territorial — that of the Jews — could actually claim the Lithuanian woods as their *haym.* It has long been recognized that Jews were prominent in the timber industry of the Russian Empire, hauling and selling lumber to the czarist authorities for railroad ties and building materials or (like Isaiah Berlin's family) exporting it west from the Baltic port of Riga. But follow the Niemen upstream a hundred years ago and you would have found Jews actively engaged at every level of the business, right down to the lumberjack colonies that dotted the river between Grodno and Kowno. My mother's family was one such clan which built a house overlooking the river, where they hauled logs from the skirts of the *puszcza Augustowska* and rafted them downstream to Kowno, using dogsleds once the river had iced over.

Given this long history, the idea of Jewish partisan bands, some of them escapees from Treblinka and the ghettos of Bialystok and Warsaw, fighting in the forests alongside the national resistance, seems less wildly improbable. But it is true that the importance of the forest mythology has been much less critical to the Jewish than to the Polish or German national memory. And had I more time, and you were unluckily captive, I could add to that list of sylvan myths and memories the English greenwood or the American wilderness (and many more), all of which, in their own way, have functioned historically as emblems of patriotic identity.

Nor, of course, is the woodland the only kind of symbolic landscape that serves this purpose of supplying an emotive topography for the "imagined community" (as Benedict Anderson has called it) of the nation. As a small child I grew up on the grimy Essex bank of the Thames estuary. Though the cockleboats of Leigh-on-Sea were nothing much to stir historical romance, even in a seven-year-old, I would look out at the sludge-brown water where the tidal river met the sea, and long before I had heard of Joseph Conrad, Rudyard Kipling, or even Arthur Bryant, would imagine it as the great artery of imperial Albion. Tilbury and Gravesend after all, were not so very far away, and I imagined Elizabeth I (much resembling Dame Flora Robson) smiting her armored breast and exhorting her troops to repel the Armada-born *tercios* (enemies alike, I noted with grim satisfaction, of Jews and Englishmen).

I hope, then, that I need not labor the significance of imagined (or indeed actual) landscapes in the psychology of national allegiance. Its most glaring instance, "America the Beautiful," was composed in an innocent time when the extension of territorial nationality was unencumbered by thoughts of those whom it displaced, still less of *their* imagined and mythical landscapes.

It is, after all, essentially an inventory of topographical blessings received like school prizes from the providential headmaster for rising to the position of Top Empire. In a darker vein, the atavistic obsessions of *Blut und Boden* persisted through the nineteenth and twentieth centuries, so that one of the most recurrent motifs in the iconography of war propaganda across the Channel was competing inspirational myths of the homelands: the sempiternal limestone village "nestling" in the Cotswolds on the one side (Frank Newbold); on the other, the copious udders of German supercows or frighteningly muscled horses hauling ploughs over what one poster artist (Werner Peine) called "the steaming furrows" of the Fatherland. As we speak here, it's difficult for us to understand the violently competing visions that, for example, Serbian Orthodox Christians, Croatian Catholics, and Bosnian Muslims have of the very same land and landscape. But of one thing we can be sure: they conflict and coincide (as do Palestinian and Israeli visions of *their* homelands) in ways programmed for disaster.

To think of the historical moment when nationalism became most obsessed with sketching its distinctive landscapes is to think automatically of the Romantics. And while, for both Polish and German history, this

Simon Schama

impression is obviously correct, the original moment when patriotic identity was imprinted with topography can be dated with some precision three centuries earlier.

For it was in the late fifteenth and early sixteenth centuries that the primitive forest was claimed as ancestral homeland. And in both cases it was taken not only *for* a people but *against* a state, namely the universalism of the Roman Empire. Around 1520, the young humanist poet Mikulaj Hussowski, the son of a forester and gamekeeper to the Jagiellonian kings, composed his extraordinary Latin poem on the Lithuanian bison, *De Statura, Feritate ac Venatione Bisontis.* The fifty-page epic was meant for the ears of Pope Leo X, an enthusiastic hunter and zoological collector. But while Hussowski's poem was evidently meant to appeal to Leo's taste for the exotic, it was not only an exhaustive description of the anatomy, behavior, and folklore of the fearsomely shaggy ungulate. It was also a eulogy for its native habitat: the barbarian forests of Lithuania, a region that had been converted to Christianity only at the end of the fourteenth century. While Hussowski was himself impeccably pious and in Rome as the protégé of a Polish prelate, his poem bragged of the primitive martial vigor of the Sarmation woods against the effete condescension of the Latins.

In this last respect Hussowski's bison poem echoed a much more famous oration by the German humanist Conrad Celtis. Celtis had also studied at the Jagiellonian University of Kraków, though he was far less taken with the Polish scenery than with its women, one of whom, the married Hasilina, inspired him to some of the most startling erotic verse of the Latin Renaissance. But it was in an address to the University of Ingolstadt in 1492 that Celtis summoned the youth of Germany to confound the conventional Italian stereotype that his countrymen were all uncultivated boors. They should henceforth, he urged, saturate themselves in poetry, art, and philosophy that they might surpass their detractors.

Defensiveness and nascent national pride are braided together throughout the Ingolstadt address. But by the time that Celtis came to lecture on Tacitus at the University of Vienna, four years later, he had gone on the offensive in his claims for the superiority of German and northern culture over the decadent, ruined south. His source, of course, was the *Germania,* the first of all Tacitus's writings to be rediscovered by the humanists (indeed by *Italian* humanists like Poggio Bracciolini and Aeneas Silvius, the Piccolomini Pope Pius II).

As Celtis well knew, the *Germania* was not merely the dispassionate ethnography of the primitive Teutonic tribes that were the perennial thorn in the side of imperial Rome during Tacitus's lifetime in the late first and early second century A.D. In many respects it was a subtle autocritique of Rome itself.

12

Germany was everything Rome was not (for better and worse). If it was rude and unpolished, it had also been uncorrupted by luxury and urbanity. If its dwellings were timbered huts rather than elegantly marbled houses and villas, those who lived in them had retained simple virtues. Their children were suckled at their mothers' breasts; they ate in common, shared property, and were quick to offer hospitality to strangers. Chastity and martial courage were second nature to them; indeed, through their wooden huts and open-air sacred groves they were still close to nature itself; were, in fact, children of nature.

Tacitus himself, at the very outset of the *Germania,* is anything but flattering to the Germans' habitat, which he describes as *silvis horrida* (bristling forests) and stinking swamps. But the generation of sixteenth-century chorographers and geographers that followed Celtis (Johannes Aventinus, Johannes Rauw, Beatus Rhenanus, and others) looked much more kindly on their native scenery. They went back to the description of the great Hercynian forest given in Pliny and Caesar, which had once extended unbroken from the Bohemerwald in the east to the Odenwald in the far northwest, and saw it as the cradle of national virtue. What these chorographers did was to adopt the old model of the civic eulogies, the *laudatii* that Italian writers like Chancellor Bruni had bestowed on Florence, and translate it not only to their native cities like Nuremberg, but to the countryside surrounding them. Aventinus actually produced what seems to have been the very first description of regional botany, and called it aptly enough the *Flora Hercynia.* The countryside they described and extolled, thick with game and the riches of the timber economy was everything that deforested Italy and the Latin south was not. And what went for topography, the German humanists implied, also went for manners and mores.

Many of the chorographies were handsomely illustrated with engravings or woodcuts, not only with maps but also evocations of the flora and fauna and local arts and crafts. But it now seems clear that the birth of autonomous landscape painting and drawing (that is to say, landscapes that had finally been freed from the dominance of sacred narrative or classical history) owed its stimulus in great part to this connection between native topography and the assertion of patriotic Christian virtue. Albrecht Altdorfer was in Vienna at exactly the time that Celtis delivered and published his lectures on Tacitus and was certainly familiar with his students and disciples. Both he and other artists in the so-called "Danube School," like Wolf Huber, produced, during the first two decades of the sixteenth century, representations of the thickly wooded coniferous forests of the Wienerwald and Boehmerwald that engaged with exactly the same definition of Germanic distinctiveness that belonged to Celtis's reinterpretation of Tacitus. Albrecht Altdorfer's woodcutter, for example, is close to the engraved representations of the primitive Germans that had already begun to feature in the new German-language editions of Tacitus. Much more important, the same artist's little *St. George,* painted on linen backed on limewood (the German medium par excellence, full of associations of the sacred and the organic), constituted a revolutionary statement against the assumptions about history landscapes that prevailed in the Latin south. Instead of a deeply recessed space, in which the narrative was organized along regular lines of perspective, Altdorfer tilted what would normally have been the horizontal background of a forest 180 degrees so that it lies as a curtain wall parallel to the picture surface. The effect of this startling move is to invert the conventional order of things, so that the ostensible action of the history is actually occluded, even strangled by the luxuriant undergrowth — an effect reinforced by the extraordinary lengths to which Altdorfer has gone to reproduce foliation. More than any other image I can think of, the panel has made the *Teutsche Bäumen* (as Boemius described them) *the* protagonist of the action.

The publication of German editions of Tacitus's great *Annals* supplied this generation of patriotic humanists with another story that defined their shared ancestry: the great battle of the Teutoburgwald in A.D. 7, when the legions of Publius Quintilius Varus were annihilated by the crudely armed soldiers of Arminius. The *Hermannschlacht* actually took place before Tacitus begins his history, and its details are only known to us through the chronicle of Velleius Paterculus, though the Romans themselves had the now-lost history of Pliny the Elder. But Tacitus's unforgettable pages (including some of the most alarming and powerful descriptions of combat ever penned) were haunted by the ghosts of Roman soldiers destroyed in the forest swamps. Indeed on the eve of a battle, their general, Germanicus, is literally visited by the nightmare of Varus's ghost rising gruesomely from the bog, one blood-spattered arm reaching out to pull him down. Before Germanicus finally prevails in A.D. 17, he has to take the battle to the woods themselves to trap the German troops with their own tactics. And even then Arminius is destroyed not by defeat but by the treachery of conspirators among his own people. Especially when compared with the conduct of Tiberius and the Roman aristocracy (the saintly Germanicus always excepted) Tacitus bestows a glowing encomium on Arminius, whom he calls, in a phrase that would be rehearsed through the centuries, the *liberator Germanies.*

The story of the *Hermannschlacht* was, of course, meat and drink to humanists in search of a founding father. And it was especially useful to Protestant rebels like Ulrich von Hutten who were unlikely to take the line of German emperors — Ottonian, Swabian, or Hohenstaufen — as suitable precedents. Arminius, on the other hand, provided a perfect *exemplum* through whom he could define Deutschtum *against* Rome, both imperial and papal. So it is not surprising to find von Hutten actually writing an *Arminius* in which he speaks through the mouth of the tribal hero.

These two traditions — of the *Hermannschlacht* in the Teutoburgwald, and of the birth of primitive virtue in the Hercynian forests — persisted through the High Renaissance and baroque period, even though they became more poeticized and classicized in the forms of their expression. But when an interest in the shared genealogy, history, and ethnography of ancient Germany revived in the mid-eighteenth century, forest scenery and the fetish of the Teutonic oak became obligatory features of patriotic topography. In Göttingen, the circle of the Hainbund (Sacred Grove) poets devoted themselves to modernized versions of what they claimed was medieval woodland lore. Enormous oaks began to figure again in elaborately allegorical paintings as the emblem of "Germania" itself, or as the ancient hiding place from which a new Barbarossa might be aroused from his long slumber. The most startlingly original of all German graphic artists of this period, Karl Wilhelm Kolbe, acquired the nickname of "Der Eiche" and used his long romantic rambles in the woods near Dessau as a starting point for etchings that explicitly recalled the woodland scenes of the Altdorfer generation, strangling isolated classical figures in massive, enveloping vegetation. Even more conventional landscapists, like the Braunschweig painter Pascha Weitsch, painted woods full of pollarded oaks near Querum not as *bürgerlich* pastorals but sacred groves. And when Georg Friedrich Kersting wanted to paint a memorial to three friends who had been killed in the *Freiheitskrieg* against Napoleon, he portrayed them in the self-consciously archaic floppy-hatted *altdeutsch* style of the *Landsturm* militia. The trio are posed in their obligatory oakwood in complementary patriotic attitudes: one upright and vigilant (the doer); another shadowed and meditative (the thinker); a third, decorated, at rest (the done-in), ready for his hero's grave.

No artist brought all these themes of patriotic topography and patriotic history together more dramatically than Caspar David Friedrich. For the tercentennial in 1823 of Ulrich von Hutten's Knights' rebellion, Friedrich provided a figure, possibly himself, dressed in a sartorial union of past and present: *altdeutsch* pseudo-Renaissance hat and coat together with nineteenth-century trousers. About him, in a forest chapel, are the graves of modern heroes of the German wars of liberation together with their forefather Arminius, von Hutten's chosen historical doppelgänger. And if the connection between ancient and modern Germany were not already sufficiently indicated, an intense dawn light illuminates a young oak rising, as that generation would say, *organically* from the tomb, while a tall fir tree provides the roof of the sepulcher — the emblems, respectively, of national and spiritual resurrection.

On and on, with relentless self-reinforcement, through the nineteenth, through the twentieth century, marched these metaphors of death and life, rot and rebirth — the olive and the oak, Roma and Germania — all the way in fact to Anselm Kiefer's materialized epic evocations of the bloodied woods of the *Hermannschlacht*. A whole series of paintings, woodcuts, and "books" created a pantheon of Germany's heroes, cultural and martial, their features made literally wooden within the grain of the timber. And it was certainly not an accident of chronology that all of the Varus-Teutoburgwald pieces were executed in the seventies, when Kiefer (whose very name, in one gender at least, means "fir tree") had come to live in the Odenwald, the westernmost arm of the old Hercynian forest.

A century and a half earlier (in the 1830s), when a monument to Hermann the German was proposed on the site of the Teutoburgwald itself (not that there was much agreement and even less evidence as to exactly where that lay), the idiosyncratic genius Karl-Friedrich Schinkel proposed a *Hermannsdenkmal* that would be mounted on a primitive rock rising literally from the German treetops of spruce and fir. The eventual structure, built by Ernst von Bandel and finally inaugurated by the Kaiser in 1875 near Detmold, is a good deal less imaginative but it too brandishes the Teutonic sword to the sky surrounded by patriotic greenery.

And while one Hermann was enshrined in stone at the western edge of the old Hercynian woods, another dreamed dreams of woodland mastery in the east. This other Hermann had the surname Goering and as virtually his first act on coming to power in 1933 had himself made *Reichsforstmeister*. As his forester-in-chief he appointed Ulrich Scherping, whose family had been royal foresters to the Hohenzollern kings and emperors. The art and the academic science of forestry had flourished in Germany as nowhere else in Europe (though there had been a brilliant, highly politicized Polish journal called *Silwa* published in Warsaw during the Congress Kingdom), but the Third Reich outdid all its predecessors in making the nationalist ecology of the *ewige deutsches Wald* an official obsession. A goodly number of forestry professors from Munich and the other major academic centers not only joined the Nazi Party but actually ended up as officers in the SS during the war along with Scherping himself. Together they helped Goering dream of a new arboreal edition of the *Drang nach Osten:* the extension of the woodlands of East Prussia, through the Lithuanian and Polish wastes, so that the whole of the northeast corner of Europe would once again be the realm of barbarian "Germania" — magnificently impenetrable, densely wooded; filled with the great beasts that Goering loved to hunt on his own estate at Rominten, elk and stag, wolf and lynx.

But most of all Goering (who mounted the most extraordinary exhibition of hunting and game trophies the world had ever seen in Berlin in

1936), wanted to hunt the *Wisent,* the great Lithuanian bison. In fact, his ambitions for eugenic design led him towards re-creating a purely Teutonic bison, and he was so confident on this score that he invited a party of diplomats to his estate at the Carinhalle east of Berlin to watch the official rutting, a tribal rite that failed to materialize on demand, the female bison trotting away in shaggy disgust as her stud made pathetic attempts at courtship.

In 1938, though, things were looking up for the *Reichsjägermeister* (for he had, of course, added this to his titles). In a desperate attempt to ingratiate themselves with the Reich, the Polish government invited the Marshal to Bialowieza. They were especially proud of the bison, which had been successfully restored to breeding stock (after the German army had eaten virtually the entire herd during the occupation of the forest in World War I). So the visit was a success. Goering slaughtered a frightening number of five-point stag, elk, bison, and boar; wallowed like a hog in the imperial bathtub that had been put in the palace lodge by Czar Alexander III; and cast a beady and covetous eye on Bialowieza itself.

In the same year, a curious facsimile edition of the manuscript of the *Germania* appeared in Berlin, photographically copied from the Codex Aesinas that belonged to Count Aurelio Baldeschi-Balleani in the Marche citadel town of Iesi. Seldom missing a chance for one-upmanship, Mussolini had shown *his* Tacito to the Führer, who lusted after the manuscript as passionately as Goering lusted for Bialowieza. The count was prevailed on to lend the precious codex for copying, but it returned to the palazzo at the beginning of the war. Only when Mussolini fell and Marche was occupied by the German army was a special detachment of SS sent to Iesi to ransack the count's palazzi in a feverish attempt to hunt down the founding document of German nationality. The classics professors with the death's-head caps failed, and the codex survived to linger on in Italy, where it is still lovingly admired from afar by German collectors.

Did Goering have better luck with the woods than Hitler with the parchment? Initially he was thwarted by the fact that in the secret partition map of Poland drawn up by the Molotov-Ribbentrop pact, Bialowieza lay firmly in the Soviet zone of occupation. Such a waste of elk! But no sooner had Operation Barbarossa been launched in 1941, than Goering had a special detachment of SS troops and police sent to secure the forest, which henceforth he annexed as his own personal domain. Scherping was installed in the hunting lodge with a corps of foresters with strict instructions to prevent the Wehrmacht from torching the woods in search of fugitives or partisans. Nothing could be done to disturb what for Goering was the perfect *Ur-wald.* On the other hand, all of its human impurities had to be relentlessly scoured so that it could be part of the great ecological remapping of the northeast woodlands. The Jews, of whom there were many thousands in the timberland economy of Bialowieza, were of course the first to go, disappearing into the Bialystok ghetto and Treblinka. Then Belorussian churches and Polish villages were sacked and burned, their inhabitants evicted en masse, with the exception of those who were allowed to remain to tend the trees and the birds and beasts of the woods — at least as long as their German counterparts needed time to supersede them.

Goering never did get to visit his new domain. And though, as an act of characteristically spiteful annihilation, German troops burned down the hunting lodges before their final retreat, they did not, perhaps significantly, touch the forest itself. It was turned over to Stalin, who was not much interested, and then to Khrushchev, who certainly was, ordering a replacement lodge of palatial dimensions to house the parties of *Nomenklatura* whom he would entertain at Bialowieza. (Needless to say, the lodge collapsed, physically, a week before it was due to open.)

Now, the marchland of the German woods has retreated in one direction (for even East Prussian villages bear Polish names), the Belorussian frontier-post is only occasionally manned, and the long presence of the Russians is marked only by the peculiar scar mown along the old border by a monstrous machine designed to preserve a bald strip in the woods where surreptitious fugitives could be seen, caught, or shot. The Poles have reclaimed the forest as their distinctively national patrimony, and the greatest and oldest oaks are named for the kings and warriors and poets of their endlessly tragic past.

There are even delicate signs of internationalism amidst all this woodland atavism, for UNESCO has finally recognized Bialowieza as a unique ecology and keeps at least a formal guardianship, watching over its priceless inventory of species already extinct elsewhere. But though the wolfpack of Bialowieza these days stalks through the snow with electronic beepers at their throats, it seems unlikely that the forest will ever be a true international ecological laboratory. It has too much history of nations that have imagined themselves inscribed in its woodland depths. There are too many memories carved (sometimes literally) on the tree-trunks; too many bodies beneath the leafmold. And even last June, when I was there, a little boy saw something old and glittering amidst the starmoss and orange boletus, and bent down to pick up a button from the Napoleonic greatcoat, a souvenir from the ancient, terrible journeys that nationalism has tracked, back and forth, in the forest depths.

Scott and the Matter of Scotland

Donald S. Carne-Ross

T HE INTRODUCTION to Walter Scott's first substantial work, *The Minstrelsy of the Scottish Border,* written in 1802–3 when he was in his early thirties, ends with these words:

> By such efforts, feeble as they are, I may contribute something to the history of my native country, the peculiar features of whose manners and character are daily melting and dissolving into those of her sister and ally. And, trivial as may appear such an offering to the Manes of a Kingdom, once proud and independent, I hang it upon her altar with a mixture of feeling which I shall not attempt to describe.

Read carefully, this passage throws a good deal of light on Scott's attitude, then and later, to the union of England and Scotland. That is, what a great if flawed novelist now lamentably little read had to say about the topic that concerns us, the worth of nations, of nationhood: whether a nation, a community of people living in the same region over a long period should, where possible, be preserved; or whether it is best submerged into some larger supranational unit.

We hear unmistakably the note of cultural loss when Scott speaks of the melting and dissolving of the manners and character of Scotland. He spoke in this way at different times throughout his life. At a meeting of the Edinburgh Faculty of Advocates in 1806, when changes in the administration of justice were being discussed he declaimed eloquently against the proposed reforms. Playfully complimented afterwards on his rhetorical powers, he burst out: "No, no — 'tis no laughing matter; little by little, whatever your wishes may be, you will destroy and undermine, until nothing of what makes Scotland Scotland shall remain." Twenty years later, in a journal entry of 1826, he wrote of the reformers: "They are gradually destroying what remains of nationality. . . . Their lowering and grinding down all those peculiarities which distinguishd us as Scotsmen will throw the country into a state in which it will be universally turnd to democracy and instead of canny Saunders, they will have a very dangerous North British neighbourhood." "If you *unscotch* us," he wrote a few days later in a letter, "you will find us damned mischievous Englishmen."

I do not think, then, that we can go all the way with Professor Hugh Trevor-Roper when he describes Scott as "one of those sensible Scotchmen [who] rejoiced in the removal of their national politics to London."[1]

But to return to the passage from the *Minstrelsy.* The peculiar features of Scottish manners and character, he wrote, "are daily melting and dissolving into those of her sister and ally," England. A peaceful, amicable dissolution, then, which Scott taught himself to see not only as inevitable but right. A disciple of the "philosophical" historians of the eighteenth-century Scottish Enlightenment, he believed in "the necessary progress of society" whereby the less civilized society or state of society must give way to the more civilized. But then the tone changes and rises as he describes his collection of ballads as "an offering to the Manes of a Kingdom, once proud and independent, [which] I hang . . . upon her altar with a mixture of feeling which I shall not attempt to describe." Here, some would say, we have Scott the romantic, vainly lamenting the passing of something that his sober best self knew *had* to pass. But the word "romantic" too easily carries a slightly or markedly pejorative note, and in due course I will suggest what I think is a better word.

Scott has often been attacked, often vehemently, by his fellow countrymen for doing what Trevor-Roper compliments him on: accepting and supporting the Union. In the belligerently nationalistic introduction to *The Penguin Book of Scottish Verse* (1970), Tom Scott wrote: "Against his own instincts and better judgment (as can be deduced from novel after novel), he took the expedient line of supporting the Union." Expediency, opportunism, compromise: these are charges that have often been leveled against Scott. Are they just? As a man, in the conduct of his affairs, he undoubtedly took full advantage of the benefits which the union with England offered to those who knew how to play their cards, and Scott played his cards very skillfully. By the age of twenty-eight, thanks to several profitable appointments, he was earning a thousand pounds a year, equivalent to fifty thousand today.

Did he also compromise as a writer? That is what matters, for if he did, his testimony to the question that concerns us must be suspect and of little worth.

We need then to turn to the novels, not to those old classroom warhorses *Ivanhoe* or *The Talisman,* but to the ten-year cycle of Scottish novels, from *Waverley* of 1814 to *Redgauntlet* of 1824. As everyone knows, Scott wrote historical novels. A better term might be societal or political, for what

1. "Scotching the Myths of Devolution," *The Times* (London), 28 April 1976.

distinguishes them is not that they are set in the past but rather that they are primarily concerned not with the novelist's usual subject matter, the interplay and analysis of personal relations, but rather with the interplay between different forms of society and the members of those societies. However, Scott almost always sets his scene in the past, for eighteenth-century Scotland was obsessed with history — "This is the historical age, and we are the historical people," Hume claimed — and this obsession lasted well into Scott's day. It is Scottish history that provided him with his subject matter and his dominant theme. The Union of the Crowns in 1603, whereby James VI of Scotland became James I of both Scotland and England; the Act of Union of 1707 by which Scotland lost its parliament: these raised the question of Scottish identity. Was Scotland to remain Scotland, or to become simply England's northern province, North Britain? And within Scotland, there was the relation between the radically different cultures of the Highlands and Lowlands. With the failure of the Jacobite rebellion of 1745, the independence and identity of the Highlands were effectively ended or, rather, brutally suppressed. An old lawless culture, yet possessed of its wild, half-savage virtues of endurance and loyalty and absolute courage, and capable of expressing itself in a grave and splendid rhetoric: all this failed as the Highlands moved towards the orderly, prosperous, civilized society south of the Highland line. To put it in another way: a noble, barbaric poetry gave way before the sober prose of the modern world. The clash of cultures, the contrast between the culture of the Highlands, always for Scott the extreme form of Scottishness — "their land is to them a land of many recollections," he wrote — and the culture of the Lowlands and England: this is the dominant theme that in one form or another inspires his best work.

In the introduction to *Rob Roy,* the fifth of the Scottish novels, Scott speaks of Rob as a man "residing on the very verge of the Highlands, and playing such pranks in the beginning of the eighteenth century, as are usually ascribed to Robin Hood in the middle ages — and that within forty miles of Glasgow, a great commercial city, the seat of a learned university. Thus a character like his, blending the wild virtues, the subtle policy, and unrestrained license of an American Indian, was flourishing in Scotland during the Augustan age of Queen Anne and George I. . . . It is this strong contrast betwixt the civilized and cultivated mode of life on the one side of the Highland line, and the wild and lawless adventures which were habitually undertaken and achieved by [those] who dwelt on the opposite side of that ideal border": Here, in Scott's own words, is his theme, which he handled with the knowledge of a historian, the analytical insight of a sociologist, and the creative powers of a great novelist. In the Scottish novels, we find this theme acted out by, and acting upon, a great array of living characters, portrayed so variously and vividly that V. S. Pritchett, a critic not drawn by training or temperament to Scott's kind of fiction, could describe him as "the single Shakespearian talent of the English novel."[2]

At his finest, Scott can show these historical, societal relations and conflicts to be as complex as those between private individuals which later novelists were to take as their subject. Nowhere more so than in *Waverley;* curiously enough, his first novel is in many ways his most subtle, and critics are nowadays inclined to think it his most accomplished.

After its leisurely opening, as readers of the book will remember, we journey with Edward Waverley into the Highlands, seeing it first through the eyes of a romantic young man steeped in "elegant literature" and enchanted to find, amid landscapes so poetic and sublime, a bona fide Scottish chieftain, Fergus Mac-Ivor, complete with picturesque clansmen and a bard who can improvise like a Homeric rhapsode. This is for Waverley quite literally a new world, one whose existence he had never suspected, unimaginably different from life on the ample English estate where he had been brought up. Gradually he comes to see, what the urbanely distanced narrator allows the reader to see far more quickly, how contrived this brilliant display of Highland manners is, cover for a carefully orchestrated political conspiracy, the Jacobite uprising of 1745. Thanks to Scott's firm historical grasp of the events he is portraying and the generosity of his temper, he can show the duplicity of the performance which Fergus is staging to gain the services of this wealthy young Englishman for the Stuart cause, and at the same time make it clear that this picture of the Highlands is not entirely false. However confusedly, Waverley is responding to something that really is or had been there, something that is missed by the ironic narrator. Both are inadequate witnesses: the reader must combine them to get at the truth. Fergus, attended by a loyal clansman to the last, faces his atrocious death heroically, the savage punishment which England reserved for traitors. He genuinely possesses the virtues he mimics. Highland society really had been as Waverley first saw it, a high barbaric culture that history had bypassed and which had to be abandoned and also honored for what was permanently valuable in it.

In *Waverley,* the contrast is between England, settled, secure, Hanoverian England, and Scotland, primarily the Highlands, making its last desperate attempt to assert its autonomy. In *Rob Roy,* written four years later, the contrast in the second, more vital, half of the novel is between the two regions of Scotland, the Lowlands represented by the canny Glasgow merchant Nicol Jarvie, and the Highlands represented by Rob Roy, a freebooter driven to his lawless yet seldom cruel way of life by economic necessity and oppression. (Scott here moves back forty years to a period just preceding the 1715 Jacobite uprising.) To many Lowlanders, the "breekless loons"

2. *The Living Novel* (New York: Reynal and Hitchcock, 1947), 56.

north of the Highland line were as alien as they were to the English, yet they both belonged to Scotland, and Scott saw it as his mission to unite them, a union that concerned him perhaps as much as the union between England and Scotland. In his novels, a critic writes, "he created an image of the Scottish past which welded the Highlands and Lowlands together in a heightened national consciousness, and made the rest of the world aware of it for the first time."[3] In *Rob Roy,* Scott points towards the possibility of such a welding, since Jarvie has Highland blood in his veins and is a relative of Rob. The time for transcending the old cultural differences has not yet come, but it is approaching. The heart of the contrast or conflict, and the possibility of its eventual transcendence, are brought out in a conversation between Jarvie and Rob which I need to quote at some length since it shows Scott the *historical* novelist at his best: that is, as Georg Lukács taught us to see, he presents a historical issue not in the way a historian does but as a novelist can do, embodying it in the relation between two vividly imagined, representative characters who experience the public issue in their daily personal lives.

> "Here are your twa sons, Hamish and Robin," Nicol Jarvie says, "whilk signifies, as I'm gien to understand, James and Robert. . . . They haena sae muckle as the ordinar grunds, man, of liberal education — they dinna ken the very multiplication-table itself, whilk is the root of a' usefu' knowledge, and they did naething but laugh and fleer at me when I tauld them my mind on their ignorance — It's my belief they can neither read, write, nor cipher, if sic a thing could be believed o' ane's ain connexions in a Christian land."
>
> "If they could, kinsman," said [Rob], with great indifference, "their learning must have come o' free will, for whar the deil was I to get them a teacher?"
>
> "Na, kinsman," replied Mr. Jarvie, "but ye might hae sent the lads whar they could hae learned the fear o' God, and the usages of civilized creatures. They are as ignorant as the *kyloes* ye used to drive to market . . ."
>
> "Umph!" answered Rob; "Hamish can bring doun a black-cock when he's on the wing wi' a single bullet, and Rob can drive a dirk through a twa-inch board."
>
> "Sae muckle the waur for them, cousin! Sae muckle the waur for them baith!" answered the Glasgow merchant in a tone of great decision; "an they ken naething better than that, they had better no ken that neither. Tell me yoursell, Rob, what has a' this cutting, and stabbing, and shooting, and driving of dirks, whether through human flesh or fir deals, dune for yoursell? and werena ye a happier man at the tail o' your nowte-bestial, when ye were in an honest calling, than ever ye hae been since, at the head o' your Hieland kernes and gally-glasses?"

Up to this point, we have two irreconcilable ways of life. "Useful knowl-

---

3. P. H. Scott in the introduction to the 1981 reprint of *The Letters of Malachi Malagrowther.*

edge" on one side, the multiplication table, reading and writing, the usages of civilized beings fortified by the fear of God. On the other, the ability to bring down a black-cock on the wing and drive a dirk through a two-inch board. But Jarvie presses his point home: What has all this violence done for you and your band of brigands? he asks. And his point strikes home, for Rob has no immediate answer. Instead, he "turned and writhed his body like a man who indeed suffers pain, but is determined no groan shall escape his lips."

> "I hae been thinking [Jarvie continues], that as it may be ye are ower deep in the black book to win a pardon, and ower auld to mend yourself, that it wad be a pity to bring up twa hopefu' lads to sic a godless trade as your ain, and I wad blithely take them for prentices at the loom, as I began mysell . . ." He saw a storm gathering on Rob's brow, which probably induced him to throw in, as a sweetener to an obnoxious proposition: "And Robin lad, ye needna look sae glum, for I'll pay the prentice-fee . . ."
>
> "Hundred thousand devils, — *Ceade millia diaoul*," exclaimed Rob, rising and striding through the hut. "My sons weavers! — *Millia molligheart!* I wad see every loom in Glasgow, beam, traddles, and shuttles, burnt in hell-fire sooner."

Jarvie gives him time to recover, and the exchange ends on a friendly note. "But ye mean weel — ye mean weel," Rob says. "So gie me your hand, Nicol, and if I ever put my sons apprentice, I will gie you the refusal o' them."

We would expect that Scott, the disciple of the "philosophic" historians of the Scottish Enlightenment, a believer in the necessary progress of society, would come out decisively on Jarvie's progressive side. He does not; he finds value in both sides. His peculiar gift was to see a past society *as it saw itself,* to see it in its own right and with its own values, not as pointing forward to some later perhaps better society. Rob Roy's clan culture, judged by standards other than its own, can only appear uncivilized and even barbaric. As such, its disappearance must no doubt be accepted but cannot be wholeheartedly welcomed, for with it the world loses virtues it can ill afford to lose.

The year 1818, which saw the publication of *Rob Roy,* also produced *The Heart of Midlothian,* a very fine book though no longer regarded by the better critics as Scott's one almost successful novel, and in 1819 came *The Bride of Lammemoor,* his only tragic novel. At this point, feeling that he had exhausted his Scottish material, he went beyond the border and far beyond his historical period and wrote *Ivanhoe,* lively enough reading to be sure, but decidedly not part of the canon.

He had not, however, said his say about the matter of Scotland and his great theme, and he returned to it in 1824 with *Redgauntlet,* which would bring the Scottish cycle to a magnificent close if the body of the book were as good as the long concluding scene. The material is in itself often admirable, but it has not been marshaled into a coherent structure. Redgauntlet is a grandiose, melodramatic figure, obviously up to something though for a while we do not see what. In due course we find that he is engaged in nothing less than the attempt single-handedly to bring about another Jacobite rebellion, twenty years after the rebellion of '45 had drawn the teeth of the Highland clans, and at a time when Charles Edward was too far gone to lead an army into battle, even if there had been an army to lead. But for Redgauntlet the house of Stuart is the symbol, by now hopelessly outdated, of a free independent Scotland.

To the historian, writing a novel about a historical event that never occurred is, I suppose, a scandalous business. Artistically, I believe that Scott was justified. The real rebellion of '45 had gone down tragically in blood. That was one possible ending, the one that actually happened. But there might have been another no less decisive ending, one that let the old heroic cause simply fizzle out, not with a bang but a whimper. This was the ending that Scott devised in *Redgauntlet,* one that required treatment in the mode of ironic comedy.

We come to see that Redgauntlet is a figure like Turnus in Virgil's *Aeneid,* the doomed opponent of the new Roman order, the *imperium sine fine* decreed by Jupiter: a noble figure for whose heroic virtues history no longer had any use. Within Virgil's Homeric structure, Turnus can be allowed his heroic status: he fights magnificently and dies tragically. But by the late eighteenth century such a figure had become utterly irrelevant, and Redgauntlet's grandiose designs are shown to be not only wrong but ridiculous. Ironic comedy is the only mode in which he can be treated, comedy sometimes close to farce and yet at times with an accent of tragic loss.

For the admirable final scene which puts paid to his ambitions, Scott assembles his entire cast. Outside, subsidiary members of the cast are brawling. Excellent comedy — we might be in the world of Tom Jones — which cannot concern us here, yet it plays an essential role in Scott's portrayal of history. Whatever momentous public issues may be taking place, he never lets us forget that ordinary people are going about their everyday business and pursuing their personal interests. Inside the inn are the reluctant conspirators Redgauntlet has brought together, members of the English nobility still professing a vestigial loyalty to the Stuart cause, but unwilling to lose their estates and perhaps even their heads in a venture which they see to be hopeless. In a back room is the aging pretender accompanied by his mistress, who is suspected of being an English spy. The conspirators beg him to get rid of her, but with typical Stuart obstinacy he will not allow that subjects have the right to make demands of a prince. They argue about what should be done, one young hothead challenges Redgauntlet to a duel on a trivial point of honor, an Oxford divine in a large academical peruke rehearses the intellectual quarrels of the previous century, boasting of his university's stand against the blasphemous tenets of Locke — and so forth. Excellent comedy again. Into this scene of embarrassed confusion briskly steps a British general in mufti, and with exquisite politeness tells them in effect to stop being silly. "His Majesty," he says, "will not even believe that the most zealous Jacobites who yet remain can nourish a thought of exciting a civil war, which must be fatal to their families and themselves, besides spreading bloodshed and ruin through a peaceful land." King George, the general continues, is more than willing to overlook this little escapade. You are all pardoned, all, without exception. Now please go home. Deeply relieved, they all prepare to do so, all except Redgauntlet. Abruptly, comedy turns to something very different. "Then, gentlemen," says Redgauntlet, clasping his hands together as the words burst from him, "the cause is lost forever!" It is indeed. An old song has ended.

This might be Scott's last word on the theme which runs through the ten-year cycle of novels. The old cause has been given a full and generous hearing, it has been honored for its bravery and its poetry and finally dismissed for its folly, whatever lingering nostalgia some might still feel for the Manes of a Kingdom once proud and independent. Scotland is henceforth to be North Britain, a peaceful, prosperous region of the kingdom ruled from London.

But there was more to come. In 1826 Scott found his personal fortune involved in and destroyed by the crash of the London money market brought about by a period of wild speculation, which left him in debt to the tune of 10,000 pounds, whatever enormous sum that amounts to in today's money. He took the disaster with great courage and resolved to pay back what he owed by his own exertions, with his pen, writing, writing, sometimes twelve hours a day in increasing ill health. Inevitably, his mood darkened, and in addition the growth of industrialism made him less certain of the material advantages of close association with the leading industrial power in the world.

Then, in the same year, something happened which brought his Scottishness, the *praefervidum ingenium Scotorum,* to the boil. This was a proposal from London that Scottish banks should no longer be allowed to issue their own notes. This was not, as it has sometimes been represented, of merely symbolic importance, for Scottish notes were an essential form of currency, and the chief means of credit in Scotland. More important, Scott saw the proposal as an example of high-handed English disrespect for Scottish interests, as though Scotland was expected to dance tamely to whatever tune London might choose to play. His feelings on the matter called forth his most vigorous piece of occasional writing, the three *Letters of Malachi Malagrowther*. (Supposedly a descendent of Sir Mungo Malagrowther, a cantankerous old Scotsman in *The Fortunes of Nigel*. Like Stendhal, Scott was given to devising fanciful aliases for himself.) The *Letters* are a passionate call, expressed often with a fine tangy humor, for Scotland to stand up for her rights, while preserving "every feeling of amity and respect towards England." There is no protest here against the Union as such, let alone any call to break violently away from it. A passage near the end of the second *Letter* shows what Scott wanted, and shows how far his ardent, generous patriotism was from the ugly nationalism that today makes many people dream of some international utopia: "For God's sake, sir, let us remain as Nature made us, Englishmen, Irishmen, and Scotchmen, with something like the impress of our several countries upon each! We would not become better subjects, or more valuable members of the common empire, if we all resembled each other like so many smooth shillings. Let us love and cherish each other's virtues — bear with each other's failings — be tender to each other's prejudices — be scrupulously regardful of each other's rights."

These admirable words might be Scott's last words, but again they are not, for in 1827 came the two late stories, "The Highland Widow" and "The Two Drovers," which are now generally held to be among his finest things, though they were not much regarded at the time. Both are tragedies, both affirm that there is something in Scotland — once again he turns to the Highlands for the extreme form of Scottishness — that is irreconcilable with England. The widow in the first of the stories had been married to a cateran, a brigand like Rob Roy who died in his blood, as a man in her view should, and she wants her only son to live and in due course no doubt die by the same wild rule. But he understands, as she does not, that a great change has taken place in the Highlands (we are now some decades after the '45): "the substitution of civil order for military violence, and the strength gained by the law and its adherents over those who were called in Gaelic song 'the stormy sons of the sword.'" Her son, however, "had perceived . . . that the trade of the cateran was now alike dangerous and discreditable, and that if he were to emulate his father's prowess, it must be in some other line of warfare, more consonant to the opinions of the present day." So he enlists in one of the Highland regiments which had been prudently formed by the British government to provide a disciplined outlet for lawless valor. When he comes home on leave, dressed in what to her is the shameful British uniform, she drugs him in order to prevent him from getting back to his unit on time. The punishment for absence without leave is scourging, and she judges that he will never submit to so ignominious a penalty. In despair, he simply waits to be arrested, but when he sees a file of redcoats coming for him, the old violence flares up again and he shoots the man in charge. He surrenders at once, is marched back, court-martialed, and shot.

The second story is no less unaccommodatingly bleak. One of the two drovers is a Highlander, the other a northern Englishman, fast friends despite their different cultures and temperaments. They quarrel in an English pub, and the Englishman knocks his friend down. Get up and fight, the English drinkers shout, but Highlanders do not fight with their fists, so he runs off to collect his dirk, returns, and stabs his friend to the heart. "He was a pretty [*gallant*] man," he says, standing over the dead body. He too gives himself up, is tried, convicted, and sentenced to death. The judge sums up in a moving, compassionate speech that brings out the cultural conflict rightly left implicit in the spare narrative. The Highlander, he explains to the jury, has acted by the terms laid down by his society, whereby a man who suffers an injury must avenge it himself, "a kind of wild, untutored justice" that English law can only condemn as murder. "I gave a life for the life I took," the Highlander says before he is hanged, "and what can I do more?"

Is *this,* then, Scott's last word? Literally, yes, in the sense that he wrote no later fictional work that expresses his theme so powerfully, but this is not the note to end on. His temper was too balanced to allow him to retain the extremism of the tragic vision for long. He saw the advantages of the Union, yet he knew that it meant the loss of something precious, the loss of a local essence that had grown slowly over a long period of time among people living in the same region, something that should never be lightly abandoned, for it cannot be replaced. Perhaps it has to go. If so, its passing must be mourned, and any, every, trace of the local essence that can be preserved must be. So I find myself once again unable to agree with Professor Trevor-Roper when he tells us that Scott "believed passionately in the Union with England."[4] He believed passionately in Scotland. He accepted and supported the Union for the political stability and material prosperity it brought to Scotland. But there are things that matter besides politics; we are not only political animals. And there are things that matter in addition to material prosperity. I do not think that we should split Scott into two, and see on one side the hard-headed disciple of the eighteenth-century Enlightenment and supporter of the Union, on the other a romantic yearning nostalgically for a past that had irretrievably gone. I do not think that we need speak of an "unresolved conflict" here, or find anything "romantic" in Scott's tenacious Scottishness. In place of Scott the romantic I propose Scott the poet, a poet whose best poetry was written in prose. Poetry has its way of holding two conflicting positions in balance, in a

4. "Sir Walter Scott and History," *The Listener,* 19 August 1971, 226.

fertile tension that preserves the rights of both. Scott took into account both the inevitability of the changes that had occurred and the losses involved. The changes had to be welcomed, or at least accepted. The losses had to be mourned, and he might well have said with his greatest poetic contemporary,

> Men are we, and must grieve when even the Shade
> Of that which once was great, is passed away.

The End of Empire in Europe

HUGH TREVOR-ROPER

I N PRAGUE, early in 1948, I met an Austro-Bohemian aristocrat whose father had been one of the last ministers of the Emperor Franz Josef, and who had himself now returned to Prague as an American journalist. The communists had not yet taken over Czechoslovakia, though they soon would. They had already imposed their rule on Poland, Romania, Bulgaria, Yugoslavia. My American-Austrian acquaintance seemed to observe the phenomenon with a tolerant or at least a dispassionate eye. "One thing that must be said for communism," he remarked, "is that it has taken the sting out of nationalism." Indeed, the fact could not be denied; and perhaps my companion's tolerance was understandable. A descendant of the Hapsburg court aristocracy, long rooted in Bohemia, might well look with some sympathy on that achievement. For Stalin had succeeded in controlling, throughout Eastern Europe, the force that had blown up the long-established multinational empire of the Hapsburgs; and nationalism, which in 1918 had been a good thing, in 1945 was a bad one.

Today that world has changed. After forty years of firm central control, forcibly, sometimes tyrannically, asserted, the uniform international communist system has collapsed, and throughout that region, from the Baltic to the Adriatic and the Black Sea, nationalism has recovered its voice, perhaps its sting. The collapse of communism has been the most extraordinary, most unforeseen event in modern times. It has ended an age, changed the face of Europe, opened new prospects. Is there any precedent for it? I think there is; for there is nothing new under the sun.

The last two centuries of European history have seen a recurrent dialectic between, on the one hand, the ideal of uniform, international order and, on the other, the claims of distinct nations become conscious of their identity and demanding recognition; and nowhere has this tension been more acute than in the lands which once formed the multinational Hapsburg empire; for there the nations have been most crowded, most fragmented, and most intermixed.

That empire had been built up, at first, piecemeal, by dynastic accident: by marriage and inheritance. It had been extended, or rounded off, in the seventeenth century, by military conquest or reconquest – Bohemia, Hungary – and in the eighteenth century by cynical, peaceful annexation – the partitions of Poland. But throughout most of this time it had been a loose, multiple monarchy whose component parts preserved their own character and institutions. Nationalism, as we know it, as distinct from traditional local loyalty or local patriotism, did not exist. That local patriotism might indeed be aroused, even inflamed, there as elsewhere, if the central government pressed too hard on the privileges or customs or interests of local societies; but the idea that each "nation," however defined – whether by race or culture or language – must be "free," must control its own living space, behind clearly defined and inclusive frontiers, and be governed by its own rulers, members of the same nation, was not yet a political truism. The political frontiers in Europe did not then seek or pretend to enclose distinct nations. Many countries contained different nations, or were ruled by foreign dynasties, which were not resented. If different societies wished to emphasize their individuality, they generally chose to do so by religious rather than political differentiation. The peoples of the Hapsburg empire, as one of their emperors would say, were "patriots for me."

Then came the first great stimulus to a new form of nationalism throughout Europe: the French Revolution. Threatened by a coalition of kings and, particularly, for sound dynastic reasons, by the Emperor, the revolutionary French Republic urged the nations of Europe to throw off their obsolete and rusty chains – the chains of monarchy and church, often foreign monarchy and international church – and establish, with French support, similar revolutionary republics: national, free republics, on classical models, with antique Roman names.

Some of them did. However, the experiment was short-lived. Having breathed, for a time, the heady air of national freedom, the new republics soon found themselves either used as counters in cynical old-style diplomacy, or converted into puppet monarchies under upstart foreign rulers drawn from the Corsican family of Bonaparte, in order to be taxed, drained, and dragooned for an imperialist war-machine. So nationalism changed sides. It became the rallying call of the resistance. The battle of Leipzig was known as the Battle of the Nations, their victory over French imperialism. Edmund Burke, the champion of an organic, stable, continuous, conservative society, on the English model, prevailed over Tom Paine, the enthusiast for the radical, rational utopianism of France; and the novels of Sir Walter Scott, which began to appear shortly before Waterloo, and which celebrated the living traditions and ancient loyalties of small countries (and one small country in particular) became the best-sellers of the European restoration.

How innocent, how romantic European nationalism then seemed! Detached from violent radical politics, it was domesticated in comfortable conservative society. If its publicist was Scott, its philosopher was Herder. Born, like Scott, far from metropolitan sophistication — in East Prussia, that detached island of Germany among the Slavs — he had been the first to preach the gospel of national identity, national culture, against the arrogant intellectual claims of the French philosophers with their insufferable condescension towards those unenlightened nations which still lagged behind them in the march of Progress. In particular, of course, Herder cried up the virtues of his own compatriots, the Germans, the heirs (as he liked to point out) of those noble savages, those robust old Nordic barbarians, who had mopped up the effete Roman ancestors of the modern Latin races, and on whose spontaneous creative vigor the artificial "paper-thin" culture of the decadent French philosophers was still based. But in spite of these *boutades,* Herder did not claim superiority for the German or indeed for any nation. To him, every nation, however small, however primitive, had its own culture, which was to be valued not by an artificial canon of "progress" or "enlightenment," imposed from outside or above, but by its authenticity; and that authenticity was expressed, above all, in its literature, its popular literature. Such literature, he insisted, the spontaneous voice of the people, was the distinctive and most precious possession of a nation; and he extolled, in particular, the ancient epics and traditional ballads now being discovered, or invented, throughout Europe: the German *Nibelungenlied,* the ancient Caledonian epic of Ossian, Bishop Percy's *Reliques of Ancient English Poetry,* and the ballads now being busily collected in Slesvig and Scotland, Scandinavia, Spain, and Greece.

In those days one really could speak of "the worth of nations." To Herder they were all worthy — all except, perhaps, the French; and the German historians, his disciples, were equally generous. The greatest of them, the founder of the new German school of historians, Leopold von Ranke, would turn aside from his work in the Venetian archives to write a history of a little country which had hardly been noticed hitherto: of Serbia. He was inspired to do so by his friend Vuk Karadjic Stefanovic, the collector of the medieval ballads of Serbia: Serbia, which was now rediscovering its national identity as it emerged, like Greece, from the long night of Ottoman conquest and domination.

This innocent, romantic, conservative nationalism, drawing on the culture and the history of the past, the nationalism of Herder and Scott, I shall designate as Nationalism Mark I. However, history does not stand still, and behind it, and drawing from it whatever nutriment it found convenient and could digest, another variety of nationalism was gathering strength: a much tougher variety, more radical, less romantic, and perhaps less innocent. It I shall designate Nationalism Mark II.

If Nationalism Mark I was a reaction against French imperialism, Nationalism Mark II had digested the lesson of that imperialism and had come to terms with it. It was comforting to feel that "the nations" of continental Europe, their individuality, their culture, had withstood the onslaught of homogenizing French imperialism, but how true was it in fact? After all, outside assistance had been necessary, and in the end, as the Duke of Wellington said, it had been "a damned close-run thing." Individually, the nations had all been defeated. Culture alone, in nations politically fragmented, could not defend itself. Herder had been, like Machiavelli's Savonarola, "a prophet unarmed." So a new generation of nationalists, in both Germany and Italy, sought to arm their culture with the protective carapace of a unitary state. And once they thought in these terms, they were brought back to Napoleon. For had not Napoleon sought to unite — and indeed partially united — Germany and Italy? Had he not re-created Poland, emancipated the Jews? In retrospect, his tyranny and executions faded from memory. In the years of the Holy Alliance he appeared as a liberal nationalist: liberalism of a kind, nationalism of a kind.

To the restored monarchical establishments of Europe this alliance of Napoleonism and nationalism was naturally disagreeable. Fortunately for them the victors of 1815 saw to it that it was kept down. They had no desire to see a revival of French revolutionary ideas, of Bonapartist adventures, of French military power; and the Concert of Europe, which had been established, was designed to prevent it. Which indeed, for over thirty years, in spite of frequent strains and occasional revolts, they contrived to do. Their ideologies and particular interests might differ, East versus West, czarist absolutism versus English constitutional monarchy, but a more general interest in preserving the settlement of 1815 prevailed — until suddenly, in one remarkable year, 1848, as if by spontaneous combustion, the whole system collapsed. Revolution broke out everywhere, spreading from capital to capital: Paris, Vienna, Berlin, Budapest, Rome; and although the intellectuals who had risen to prominence in the hour of revolution — a Lamartine, a Kossuth, a Mazzini — were soon pushed aside and ultimately the old rulers, somewhat chastened, crept back, their world would never be quite the same. It was a breakthrough — "the springtime of the nations" — a return to Napoleonism, a neo-Napoleonism, "a Napoleonism without Napoleon," it has been called; and soon, in fact, it would have a Napoleon too, "Napoléon le Petit," Napoleon III, who, being conscious of his pedigree, would set out to realize *les idées napoléoniennes.* He would offer himself as the patron of revolutionary nationalism throughout Europe, the champion of German and Italian unity, in whose contradictions he would duly become entangled, and by which, in the end, he would himself, an unskillful engineer, be blown up.

Plus ça change, plus c'est la même chose. Have we not seen this scenario repeated in our time? An uneasy balance of power established after a long war and designed, above all, to prevent the revival of a defeated military and ideological power which had recently dominated the continent; nationalism, by that balance, held in check; occasional outbreaks — East Berlin 1953, Budapest 1956, Prague 1968 — all contained; and then, after many years and the emergence of a new generation, the *dégringolade:* the sudden collapse of the old order in one capital after another, the revival of nationalism, sometimes even in frightening form — for 1815 read 1945; for 1848, 1989.

The nationalism which broke through in 1848, and which I have called Nationalism Mark II, was political nationalism: the demand that the nation, and the culture which gives it its identity, its individualism, its life, must have its own state, as a necessary protective shell; and that this state must be coextensive with the nation, organically part of it, its natural integument. So Germany, a new, united German state, must contain all Germans, all who represent German culture. Germany, which had been defined — in the years when it had no politics, being politically fragmented, when only culture united it — as a *Kulturvolk,* must become a *Kulturstaat.* Similarly Italy, a newly united Italian state, must contain all Italians: the petty princes, who had symbolized its division, must be swept aside. Such political nationalism entailed economic nationalism too; the removal of the old internal frontiers would create a new national market, as in postrevolutionary France. Thus cultural idealism merged with commercial realism, the aspirations of intellectuals with the interests of the bourgeoisie.

Between 1848 and 1870 German and Italian unity was achieved. It was achieved at the expense of the old regime, restored in 1815, and especially at the expense of the multinational Hapsburg Empire, the victim alike of German and of Italian nationalism. But why should the process stop there? Germany and Italy might claim priority. They were "historic nations" even when divided. But was not Poland also a historic nation, once a great united kingdom, only recently divided? And what of Hungary and Bohemia, also historic kingdoms? All these, if they secured their ancient freedom, must do so at the expense of the Hapsburg Empire. And once they had shown the way, were there not other, smaller nations, which might also assert themselves, even against these "historic nations" — Croats in Hungary, Vlakhs in Transylvania — or against another great multinational empire, also now much weakened, the Ottoman Empire: Serbia, for instance, Vuk's Serbia, with its national ballads, Greece, with its great past — these had already staked out their claims; Bulgaria with its memories of a medieval empire; Romania with its warrior princes and antique Roman claims. All these were now lining up on the waiting list for national self-determination, and great powers, in their own interest, were prepared to back their claims.

But if all these new nations were to assert themselves, and claim political as well as cultural identity, where were their national frontiers to be drawn? In the past, the question had not arisen. Frontiers had then been one thing, nations another: they had been formed separately, by separate forces, and there was no necessary coincidence between them. Most frontiers were traditional, some of great antiquity. If they had been adjusted, it was generally by war or treaty: nationality, or culture, or language did not come into it. And nations equally had found their living space without reference to frontiers, new or old: they settled where they could. Especially in Eastern Europe. There successive waves of immigration, conquest, colonization — Hungarian and Slav, Tartar and Turk, Swedish and German — had flowed over the land, leaving pools and pockets and superimposing layers of population, some large, some small, for which no precisely defined frontiers existed or could rationally be devised. When such nations became conscious of their nationality and sought to define it in new terms and demand exclusive political frontiers, what insoluble problems were created! On the open eastern shore of the Baltic Sea cultures were superimposed, layer upon layer, Swedish, German, Russian, over the native base. In Hungary the Magyars themselves were a minority, ruling over Vlakhs, Ruthenians, Croats, all now looking towards their kinsmen across the established frontiers of the kingdom. No wonder some of these peoples, when the implications became clear, drew back, preferring the protection of distant traditional rulers to an uncomfortable independence at the mercy of oppressive rivals close at hand: that a Croatian general in imperial service should crush the Hungarian rising in 1848; that a Czech patriot, František Palacký, should declare that if the Hapsburg Empire did not exist, it would be necessary to create it; and that, short of emigration to a Zionist utopia, the Emperor should seem the best guarantor of the Jews in Austria.

After 1918, when the First World War — precipitated though not caused by these problems — had ended in the crash of four great empires, Nationalism Mark II achieved its triumph. The Western victors, finding themselves suddenly unchallenged arbiters of Europe, applied its principles and sought, within the imperatives of politics, to satisfy the claims of the nations. They would create a Europe of nation-states, defined by culture and language. Although their attempts have often been ridiculed as ill-informed or unrealistic, they did not do so badly: the frontiers which they drew, though contemptuously canceled by Hitler and Stalin, have now, to a large extent, been restored. The error of the West was not in the frontiers which it then drew, but in its failure to provide for their preservation when the defeated great powers had recovered their strength, and that new strength was directed by a new form of nationalism, Nationalism Mark III.

For in one respect, the statesmen of 1918 did not apply their own principles. Indeed they could not, for the problems were insoluble. So, naturally enough, they penalized the aggressor. Where national claims conflicted, those of Germany were rejected. It was the penalty of defeat; but it bred a terrible revenge. Just as the innocent cultural nationalism of Herder, after the defeat of Jena, had been fortified by the hard carapace of political power, so the political nationalism which had replaced it, and had now in turn been defeated, was reanimated by the injection of a terrible new intoxicant. From political it became racial.

It is Hitler's achievement to have discredited every idea which he took up by expressing it, and applying it, in its most extreme form. Nationalism Mark I, nationalism defined by culture, had entailed no hierarchy of values: German culture was not superior to other cultures, provided that they too were authentic. Absolute standards were rejected together with the patronizing French Enlightenment. Nationalism Mark II changed that. Once national culture was identified with state power, hierarchy returned, for some states were clearly more powerful than others. So culture would be measured by power, and as German power grew, so did the claims of its culture. After 1870 this was a German truism, against which Burckhardt and Nietzsche vainly protested. The war of 1914 was declared a war for German culture. Even so, nationalism — at least the nationalism of small nations — was still a liberal cause. But when Hitler redefined the nation as the race, and measured its culture by its blood, the whole concept of "the worth of nations" was degraded. A new way lay open, and in due course the smaller nations would explore it too. Herder's romantic barbarians would resort to the gas chambers of Auschwitz, Vuk's Serbian folk heroes to "ethnic cleansing," and nationalism would become a dirty word.

How did this last change — the fusion of the idea of nationality with the concept of race and a hierarchy of races — come about? Let us not pursue so difficult a question. Precedents can be found for anything. The belief in the superiority of a particular race has a long pedigree. So does anti-Semitism, though its rationalization has changed. The concept of "purity of blood" — and the impurity of Jewish blood — was a truism in sixteenth-century Spain. The idea of the inequality of races was formulated by a lightweight French aristocrat in the mid–nineteenth century. But the fusion of these ingredients with aggressive German nationalism occurred, logically enough, in the place where the races themselves were most inextricably intermixed, in the multinational Hapsburg empire. There the nationalism of the Austrian Germans was sharpened and turned inwards by the successive defeats of 1858 and 1866 and the economic crisis of the 1870s. It was there that Hitler learned the ideology which became, in his own words, "the granite foundation" of his thinking, and which he would afterwards carry with him to another German nation, also defeated, also in economic crisis, on ground prepared to receive it.

So today, when we see the collapse of another great multinational empire, held together for seventy years by an international, antinational ideology, and apprehend a revival of the nationalism whose "sting" it could claim to have removed, what kind of new nationalism do we expect to see? Pessimists think of the last stage, Nationalism Mark III: the rabid nationalism and anti-Semitism which has discredited the whole idea. But perhaps we should not look at the worst scenario. Perhaps, if we go back to a truer definition of nationality, if we expel the total doctrine of racialism, which has no basis in biology, and do not demand too rigid frontiers in a continent of many nations, we may recover the innocent cultural variety of Herder and in the *Europe sans frontières* promised in 1993 achieve the ideal of General de Gaulle, to which I gladly subscribe: a *Europe des patries.*

Lessons of History?

BEN WHITAKER

I AM GREATLY HONORED to be asked to participate in this distinguished *conversazione* in the famous intellectual mosaic of Boston. It was in Boston in 1860 that Wendell Phillips declared, "Governments exist to protect the rights of minorities. The loved and the rich need no protection — they have many friends and few enemies." Today arguments whether national, religious, or ethnic groups' interests are best pursued by federation or fission have achieved new urgency, not least as we saw in the British Parliament last week. Even before the end of the Cold War opened a Pandora's box, in Eastern and Central Europe, of causes and conflicts that had been muted or suppressed by the ideological struggle, there had been, from Quebec and Lombardy to inside Belgium, a revival of political thinking that "smaller is more beautiful," perhaps as a feeling of reaction against the impersonality of government by such distant bureaucracies exemplified by the European Community or the former Soviet Union. Although in the United Kingdom we all, including separatists, are at present clinging together trying to bail out the same economic lifeboat, the United Nations Secretary General has recently expressed fears that unless new political policies are adopted and the rights of minorities moved to the top of the international agenda, the world may splinter into four hundred economically crippled mini-states, while his own continent of Africa could revert into its five thousand constituent tribal territories, which had previously been arbitrarily divided or forced together by lines drawn on maps by European imperial powers.

Before considering the desirability or otherwise of this scenario, it is worth taking a glance at the exceptions to these fissiparous tremors, such as the United States and Switzerland. I am not so foolhardy as to try to venture here any views about the former, but Switzerland (despite its four national languages) remains, I suggest, an oasis of tranquil stability, partly because it is surrounded by several more powerful neighbors. Many other nations need to invent barbarians at the gates — especially where the nations' governments are themselves barbaric. Perhaps the only thing which might reunite Yugoslavia today might be if some larger power could be persuaded to threaten it with attack. I remember from the days when I was briefly a minister in the British Government and we were in despair — as all such governments habitually are — about Northern Ireland, one of the few fresh ideas was to send a joint Arab-Israeli peacekeeping force there, in the hope this might have the effect of uniting all the Irish population shoulder-to-shoulder together against it.

Each nation's ethnic or religious amalgam of course is distinct historically, geographically, socioeconomically, and psychologically. But *The Economist* recently suggested that, in considering whether present national boundaries should be sacrosanct or ethnic groups achieve new separate self-determination, three tests should be applied: First, are there recent memories of ethnic slaughter? Second, have recent borders left a difficult ethnic muddle? And third, is another powerful country interested to the point of intervention?

The twentieth-century history both of Armenia and of Ireland, unhappily, qualify under each of these heads. The modern national identity of Armenians is partly forged by the memory of the genocidal slaughter, by the Ottoman Empire in 1915, of at least 600,000 and possibly 1 million out of the Armenian population of 1.8 million. While the country of Armenia itself is situated (symbolically, perhaps, on an earthquake fault line) between the rock of Russia and the hard place of Turkey, the fact that the Armenian enclave of Nagorno-Karabakh is totally cut off and surrounded inside Azerbaijan, which has religious and other links with Turkey, keeps alive Armenian fears that Turkey may again intervene.

About the problem of Ireland — the continuing effects of its *damnosa* legacy of tragic historical memories and its literally indefensible current northern boundary — it is otiose to need to say much in Boston, except perhaps to observe that sometimes the power of myth is greater than that of history: few of the paramilitary gunmen in the Falls or Crumlin Roads may be aware that orange historically used to be the color of the Roman Catholics, or that the pope in fact supported King William at the Battle of Boyne. Ireland's "double minority" dilemma, deeply rooted in the psychological tensions of group identity and insecurity, is of course due to political and socioeconomic issues rather than the religious one to which it is usually simplistically ascribed. But the continuing impasse about Northern Ireland regrettably exemplifies the limitations of an ex-imperial power in settling the future of its former territories. Although such a power can strive for impartiality, as Britain did between Hindus and Muslims when relinquishing India; and although the able current and recent Secretaries of State for Northern Ireland have presided patiently, year after weary year, over dialogues of the deaf at constitutional talks about the Northern Irish problem; it is incontrovertible that history disqualifies Britain from being viewed as impartial by many Irish people. Carson exploited the British government's political vulnerability at the time of the First World War to make it renege on its promise of an independent united Ireland; and the fact that today the Ulster Unionist MPs often hold the balance of power at Westminster does not argue well for a successful settlement to the constitutional talks — which a few days ago were once again suspended in failure. Hence the first of my conclusions, that if the boil is to be lanced here (as has also recently been shown in Bosnia or Somalia), some international input — whether by the European Community, the UN, or President-elect Clinton's deus ex machina — is necessary as an alternative to civil war or terrorism.

If we do not learn from history, we have been warned, we are condemned to repeat it; but we seem somewhat slow students. If the international community had learned from and taken action on the 1915 genocide of the Armenians by the Ottomans, which significantly was assisted by technical experts from their then-ally Germany, we might have preempted the later Holocaust of Jews and others, not least because prototype gas chambers, concentration camps, and inhumane medical experimentation were practiced against the Armenians. Hitler, with chilling significance, is reported to have said, "Who now remembers the Armenians?" The fact that, in contrast to the postwar German government's responsible attitude towards the Nazi crimes, the Turkish government still does not admit what occurred, again confirms that some supranational dimension is essential in the protection of the human rights of ethnic groups. Such guarantees of human rights might help make some vulnerable groups to feel securer, before a recourse to conflict or demands for secession escalate. But these guarantees would need to be backed by credible international sanctions and peacekeeping forces: "ethnic cleansers" are scarcely likely to be deterred by a few clauses in a constitution.

Yugoslavia today clearly illustrates the flaw inherent in the right to self-determination, which is that a group which secedes can often intensify the fears of other minorities contained in it. This "sorcerer's apprentice" characteristic of nationalism was eloquently delineated by Shakespeare in the little-known play *Sir Thomas More,* which he coauthored, when More says to the anti-immigrant English xenophobes of that day:

> Grant them remov'd, and grant that this your noise
> Hath chid down all the majesty of England;
> Imagine that you see the wretched strangers,
> Their babies at their backs, with their poor luggage,
> Plodding to th'ports and coasts for transportation,

And that you sit as kings in your desires,
Authority quite silenc'd by your brawl,
And you in ruff of your opinions clothed,
What had you got? I'll tell you. You had taught
How insolence and strong hand should prevail,
How order should be quell'd — and by this pattern
Not one of you should live an aged man;
For other ruffians, as their fancies wrought,
With selfsame hand, self reasons and self right
Would shark on you, and men like ravenous fishes
Would feed on one another.

(act 2, scene 6)

Conor Cruise O'Brien, among others, has persuasively argued that human rights are best thought of as inherent in each human being, irrespective of what kind of cultural grouping he or she may belong to: "The culture of a group may include systematic violations of human rights. When we are told to respect the cultures of groups we are being told to respect things which may include for example the Hindu caste system, the treatment of women in Islam." I've no doubt that Salman Rushdie for one would agree. This is why the UN Universal Declaration of Human Rights always prefers to speak of the rights of individuals and not of groups. Of course, such individual rights include the right not to suffer any disadvantages through being a member of a minority. But devolved power did not lead to greater toleration either in the Old South of the United States, nor when Northern Ireland was self-governing. Since so many national governments have shown themselves incapable of safeguarding such rights — even when democratically elected (as we should remember Hitler himself was) to exert "the tyranny of the majority" — a radically reconstituted international capacity to protect is essential.

The UN has recently clearly established the precedent, in Cambodia, Yugoslavia, Kuwait, and some of the Kurdish territories, that it can intervene, within nation-states, in the higher interests of peace and human rights. There are today calls for it to enforce electoral results in Angola, Haiti, and Burma, and to help Tibet and East Timor to self-determination. The concept that sovereignty is sacrosanct will, in any event, increasingly be eroded in an age where major environmental threats pay no respect to national boundaries. A reformed and strengthened United Nations is overdue that can truly serve the needs of "We the peoples of the world," as asserted in the opening words of its charter, rather than those of "We the governments of the world," as is the case in its present corrupt version. (A start could be made by making it a condition that a country, before it can vote at the UN, must [a] have paid any arrears of money it owes the UN, and [b] have its government democratically elected.) Otherwise we will continue to allow a premium to be put on *force majeur* or terrorism. For what it is worth, my own prediction is that our children will grow up in a world of more limited sovereignties — where sovereignty is increasingly shared, with economic and other federations above and internal government devolved to regional units, and overall, I hope, an enhanced international authority.

The day of "my country, right or wrong" is, I hope, dying. Patriotism, liable to be the last refuge of scoundrels, is not enough. Although it can, at its best, express a selfless sense of collective responsibility, nationalism, as Richard Aldington has described, is "a silly cock crowing on its own dunghill." Whether writ large or small, nationalist emotions are too easily exploited by unscrupulous demagogues as a diversion from society focusing on its real ills and injustices. Northern Ireland is a classic example of where the proper and essential political debate about social issues has been completely stymied for seventy years by the tribal feuding.

Ethnocentric education has caused historical ghosts and grievances to be refought over by innocent victims today. Few impartial authorities doubt that the right of parents to educate their children in separate religious schools in, for example, Northern Ireland has contributed to the blind hostility exhibited by many of the communities there. Language recently seems to be dividing rather than helping Canadians to communicate. Gandhi said civilization should be judged by its treatment of minorities. I suggest that the decision whether to integrate or assimilate should be a matter for the individual, not the group — though for any such a choice to have reality requires that both options are available to her or him. As a wise Irish writer, the late Hubert Butler, summed it up: "It is as neighbors, full of ineradicable prejudices, that we must learn to love each other, and not as fortuitously separated brethren."

Transcending the Nation's Worth

Liah Greenfeld

ABOUT A CENTURY AND A HALF AGO, during the time which was called "the spring of the nations," when nationalism seemed to be the ruling passion on the continent of Europe, daily strengthening its grip on the hearts and minds of people, young Karl Marx asserted in the "Manifesto of the Communist Party" that the days of nationalism and nations were counted. He wrote:

> The bourgeoisie has through its exploitation of the world-market given a cosmopolitan character to production and consumption in every country.... it has drawn from under the feet of industry the national ground on which it stood. All old-established national industries have been destroyed or are daily being destroyed. They are dislodged by new industries, whose introduction becomes a life and death question for all civilized nations, by industries that no longer work up indigenous raw material, but raw material drawn from the remotest zones; industries whose products are consumed, not only at home, but in every quarter of the globe. In place of the old wants, satisfied by the productions of the country, we find new wants, requiring for their satisfaction the products of distant lands and climes. In place of the old local and national seclusion and self-sufficiency, we have intercourse in every direction, universal inter-dependence of nations...."[1]

Marx's argument, in short, was that the speedy and imminent demise of nationalism was made inevitable by the globalization of economy implied in the spread of capitalism.

In the 1990s this same assertion and the same argument are gaining new popularity. Nationalism, we hear, is a dying phenomenon; it is in a long-time inevitable decline; the time of nations has passed, their worth transcended, for they have outlived their — essentially economic — purpose.[2]

---

1. "Manifesto of the Communist Party," in *The Marx-Engels Reader,* 2nd ed., ed. Robert C. Tucker (New York: Norton, 1970), 476–77.
2. Eric Hobsbawm's *Nations and Nationalism Since 1780* (Cambridge: Cambridge University Press, 1990) is perhaps the most famous recent example of this view.

As in 1848, what we see offers little to justify such an assertion. A new "spring of the nations" seems to be upon us, new nations springing up wherever one turns, and after another revolution, nationalism appears to be the ruling passion on the continent of Europe. This is not to say that it rules within every heart or even within the hearts of the overwhelming majority of Europeans, but only that, as a collective sentiment, it certainly has no rivals. It is safe to say that nationalism transcends the worth of its universalistic alternatives, whether of the liberal or of the socialist variety. And the conservative alternatives to nationalism have been dead — and, I would propose, forgotten — for at least a century. But, as in 1848, we doubt what we see.[3]

In itself, the continuing vitality of nationalism is, obviously, not a convincing argument against the assertion of nationalism's imminent demise. "Imminent" is a relative concept; the believers in nationalism's doom have persisted in their belief for a century and a half, undaunted by the show of this vitality (in fact, the persistence of nationalism has been at least matched by the persistence of the belief in its speedy disappearance); and if we wait long enough, perhaps we'll see nationalism disappear. But I have only half an hour or so, so I am told, to present my view, and I cannot afford to wait.

The fact is that the nation's worth has not been transcended yet. For that reason the question when and under what conditions it may be transcended cannot be answered empirically. But, empirical resolution pending, seeing or not seeing in the present signs that the nation's worth is being transcended depends on one's interpretation of the nation and one's understanding of the basis for its worth in the first place.[4]

A nation is a historically recent phenomenon. It, in other words, had no worth for most of human history. What made it worthwhile? I beg to differ with the prevalent view that nationalism is a functional requirement of industrialization, called forth by the needs of industrializing economy and political structure that it makes possible or necessary.[5] My reason for doing

3. Those who believed what they saw, rather than what the logic of the globalization argument implied, pointed to the fact that economic unification of the world not only did not result in spiritual unity, but coincided with its very destruction. Tocqueville wrote: "It is not, I think, going too far to say that in the fourteenth century the political, social, administrative, judicial, and financial institutions — and even the literary productions — of the various European countries had more resemblance to each other than they have even in our time, when the march of progress seems to have broken down all barriers and communications between nations have so vastly improved." See *The Old Regime and the French Revolution* (1856), trans. Stuart Gilbert (Garden City, N.Y.: Doubleday, 1955), 16.

4. This presentation repeats, in brief, several of the arguments I made in *Nationalism: Five Roads to Modernity* (Cambridge: Harvard University Press, 1992). The format of the conference, however, makes it possible only to mention these arguments and does not allow their elaboration.

5. Ernest Gellner, *Nations and Nationalism* (Oxford: Basil Blackwell, 1983). Hobsbawm, *Nations and Nationalism Since 1780*.

so is that, historically, industrialization was preceded by the emergence of nationalism. For the same reason of historical precedence I beg to differ from another widespread view—that nationalism, which may be considered a functional equivalent of great religions, is (or was) a functional requirement of secularizing societies.[6] Nationalism emerged in the time of ardent religious sentiment, when questions of religious identity grew more, rather than less, acute than before, and faith more significant—the time of the Reformation. It was able to develop and become established owing to the support of religion, and, if it later replaced it as the governing passion, in many cases it incorporated religion as a part of national consciousness.

The worth of the nation—the psychological gratification afforded by national identity and therefore its importance—I would claim, is related to the experience of dignity by wide and ever widening sectors of humanity. Nationalism originated as a reaction—one of many possible reactions—to the structural contradictions of the society of orders. It was a response of individuals in elite sectors of society, who were personally affected by these contradictions and were placed by them in a state of status-inconsistency. The inventors of nationalism were members of the new—Henrician—aristocracy in England. Upwardly mobile commoners, who reached the top of the social ladder, they found unacceptable the traditional image of society in which social mobility was an anomaly, and substituted for it a new image, that of a *nation* as it came to be understood in modern times. When this happened, the word "nation" meant something entirely different; it referred to a political and cultural elite, rather than to a society as a whole. Henrician aristocrats, however, made it synonymous with the "people" of England, a concept which—in English as in other European languages—referred specifically to the lower orders, the rabble or plebs, as members of which so many of them were born. As a result of this inspired redefinition (for it was a matter of inspiration, in no way inevitable and therefore in no way predictable) every member of the people was elevated to the dignity of the elite, becoming, in principle, equal to any other member. The remarkable quality of national identity which distinguishes it from other identities—and also its essential quality—is that it guarantees status with dignity to every member of whatever is defined as a polity or society. It is this quality that recommended nationalism to European (and later other) elites whose status was threatened or who were prevented from achieving the status they aspired to; that ensured the spread of nationalism throughout the world in the last two centuries; and that explains its staying power in the face of the economic interests that ostensibly pull in the other direction.

6. Benedict Anderson, *Imagined Communities,* 2nd ed. (London: Verso, 1991).

I would not claim, as does Francis Fukuyama, that the experience of dignity (or social recognition) is essential to human life, since during most of recorded history most men and women lived without dignity. It is not status attainment, but status maintenance (which applies to low status as much as to high status) which is essential, and during most of human history only high status (that is a very small minority of social positions) was associated with dignity. Yet, dignity is addictive: having known it, one can no longer be happy without it. Who better to quote in support of this claim than the founding father of the discipline of economics and the author of *The Wealth of Nations*, Adam Smith, who (however disagreeable this may be to those who see in him the advocate of the primacy of economic factors) considered status to be "the cause of all the tumult and bustle, all the rapine and injustice, which avarice and ambition have introduced into this world." Dignity, says Smith, "when once it has got entire possession of the breast, will admit neither a rival nor a successor. To those who have been accustomed to the possession or even to the hope of public admiration, all other pleasures sicken and decay."[7]

It is safe to assume that in modern society people will never agree to be deprived of the dignity which they acquired with nationality. The possibility of transcendence of the nation's worth, therefore, depends on the availability of alternative guarantees of dignity, on finding (or inventing) a functional equivalent of nationality in this respect.

In the early days of nationalism, different elite groups which were exposed to nationalist ideas reacted differently to them, in accordance with the relative ability of nationalism to aid them in their status-maintaining and status-aggrandizing pursuits. An interesting example is furnished by the nobility in various German lands who as late as the early nineteenth century remained indifferent to the appeal of nationalism, embracing it rather reluctantly during the Wars of Liberation. Throughout the eighteenth century, when the French and the Russian nobilities converted to nationalism *en masse,* and until the defeats at the hands of Napoleon, the German nobility enjoyed undisturbed social ascendency. It was content, its status was as exclusive as ever, and there was no reason why it would welcome anyone else to partake in it. The nation had no worth for this nobility, nationalism could offer it nothing. In both France and Russia, in distinction, the status of the nobility was threatened, its exclusivity long gone and its dignity, therefore, devalued; in both countries nobles felt humiliated by the central power and deprived of any power of their own. It was thus worthwhile for them to discard the old — estate — identity, which bred expectations of dignity but no longer provided means to satisfy them and

7. Adam Smith, *The Theory of Moral Sentiments,* ed. D. D. Raphael and L. A. Macfie (Indianapolis: Liberty Classics, 1982), 57.

so condemned one to a life of frustration and fear that whatever remained of one's status would be lost, and adopt a new — national — identity, which redefined the nobility's relations with the central power and guaranteed status and dignity. As far as the German nobility was concerned, nationalism was not able to transcend the worth of the society of orders; for the French and the Russian nobilities it successfully transcended this worth.

In the case of non-noble intellectuals (the second of the two elite groups that was responsible for the initial establishment of nationalism in Europe), the idea of the nation also had to compete with other status-bestowing frameworks, and so long as other identities appeared to promise more dignity, failed to captivate them and secure their commitments. French philosophes were above particularistic self-content. Voltaire thought that "a philosopher has no *patrie* and belongs to no faction" and that "every man is born with the natural right to choose his *patrie* for himself." Abbé Raynal believed that "the *patrie* of a great man is the universe." Great men, explained Duclos, "men of merit, whatever the nation of their origin, form one nation among themselves. They are free of puerile national vanity. They leave it to the vulgar, to those who, having no personal glory, have to content themselves with the glory of their countrymen."[8] So long as one could reasonably hope to become world-famous (and French philosophes in the mid–eighteenth century still had a reasonable chance of that), it was foolish to limit oneself to a small part of the world; and if one was confident in one's superiority and felt assured of recognition, one had no need of the shared dignity of a nation. In fact, one had no need of nation at all; *republic of letters* was enough.

Ironically, at the very time when French philosophes dismissed the nation as too small for their grand designs and exhibited such confidence in their ability to win the hearts of audiences — and therefore prestige — everywhere, and perhaps to no small degree owing to this confidence, audiences everywhere (at least in Europe) were closing their hearts to them, making such conquests very difficult and the nation the only place where one could reasonably hope to make them.

Another reason why French eighteenth-century intellectuals were hesitant about nationalism was the fact that, as a result of the crisis and the redefinition of the nobility, the latter opened its doors to talent, and for low-born luminaries noble status was dignified enough. It was nobility's giving up on itself that eventually persuaded many of them to give up their hope of joining the nobility and turn national patriots instead.

---

8. Voltaire, "Réflexions sur l'histoire," in *Oeuvres complètes* (Paris: Garnier Frères, Libraires–Editeurs, 1879) 25:170; "Annales de l'empire," 13:513. Guillaume Thomas Raynal, *Histoire philosophique et politique des établissements et du commerce des Européens dans les deux Indes* (Geneva: Chez les Libraires Associés, 1775) 5:10. Charles Pinot Duclos, *Considérations sur les moeurs de ce siècle,* in *Oeuvres diverses* (Paris: Dessesartes, 1802) 1:10. Greenfeld, *Nationalism,* 156.

German nationalism was a later development than the French, and German intellectuals remained faithful to their cosmopolitan ideals long after their French brethren abandoned theirs. Nicolai considered German nationalism "a political monstrosity"; Schiller claimed to have lost his fatherland "to exchange it for the great world" and wrote "as a citizen of the world." Fichte was a principled cosmopolitan as late as 1799. When, accused of atheism, he lost his professorship at Jena, he hoped for French victory in Germany (for nothing was more certain to him "than the fact that unless the French achieve the most tremendous superiority [in Germany], no German who is known for ever having expressed a free thought will in a few years find a secure place") and asked to be employed by the French Republic.[9] Nationalism lacked an appeal to German intellectuals before the Napoleonic campaign because they were the only group interested in the redistribution of prestige in society, and, without the support of the nobility and the bureaucracy, they lacked the means to enforce it. To insist on such a redistribution (implied in the idea of the nation) in this situation would only invite ridicule and damage the chances of social advancement some of them had. It was more satisfying to dream that one was an equal member of a community of intellectuals and hope for the recognition of that community (even though in the case of German intellectuals such a hope in the eighteenth century was not reasonable) — for this at least would not be laughed at. Nationalism was irrelevant and the nation worthless. The French invasion made it worthwhile. It created a community of interest between the intellectuals and the higher classes, who, so prohibitive and inaccessible before in their superiority, now allowed the intellectuals, in fact welcomed them, to take part in their worries and sorrows. What the nobility and the intellectuals shared, and what made the nobles look favorably on intellectuals, was that they were Germans. While cosmopolitanism and the idea of a world intellectual community offered German intellectuals a form of escape, a possibility to dream about social fulfillment and advancement, partnership in a nation offered real possibilities of such advancement.

The argument that the nation's worth varies in accordance with the possibilities for dignified status it offers is supported, among other things, by the fact that, in those rare cases in modern history when the nation's worth was transcended (whether permanently or, as the case mostly was, temporarily), such transcendence had very little to do with economy and everything with status.

The architects of nationalism everywhere, people who came up with, articulated, and popularized new ideas, were, unavoidably, intellectuals —

9. G. P. Gooch, *Germany and the French Revolution* (New York: Russell and Russell, 1966), 33–34. Hans Kohn, "The Paradox of Fichte's Nationalism," *Journal of the History of Ideas* 10 (June 1949), 321 n. 5.

articulators and disseminators of ideas, by definition — whether professional or not and whatever their social origins. In some important cases, however, this crucial role was played by professional intellectuals, and in these cases professional intellectuals were rewarded by (or, rather, secured for themselves) high social status for generations to come. They became the new aristocracy. Like the latter, they do not have to be particularly wealthy and, as a rule, do not have much power, but they enjoy great prestige, and they enjoy it because they are intellectuals. Nationality may be more worthwhile for intellectuals than for others, and this explains why, as a matter of fact, intellectuals are very rarely alienated from their societies. Often, they may be antiestablishment and opposed to their governments, because they may not like these governments' policies and believe that they know better, but they are not, as a rule, opposed to their nations. For that reason, they very rarely emigrate, unless forced to do so.

But there are exceptions to this rule, and these exceptions help to underscore conditions under which the nation's worth may be transcended. By exceptions I do not mean individuals (there are always exceptional individuals), but societies. One such exception is the United States of America. Here, professional intellectuals did not play a central role in the articulation of national consciousness, because they did not exist as a group until perhaps the 1830s. For this, as for several other reasons, American intellectuals have not enjoyed the great prestige and authority enjoyed by intellectuals in France, Germany, or Russia (and it is possible that even in England, where the situation is quite similar to the American, intellectuals enjoy greater respect). American intellectuals were never recognized as an aristocracy in this society which took democracy more seriously than others (for it was, indeed, ingrained in its national consciousness) and recognized no aristocracies whatsoever. Both wealth and power carry more independent weight in America than in any European society, and status is highly correlated with wealth and power, which is not as general a rule in Europe. ("It is better to be *nouveaux riches* than no *riches* at all," says an inscription on an etching by a Cape Cod artist, Carol Lummis. New money, that is, money not tied to previous status, carries no stigma in this country. An etching with an inscription "It is better to be no *riches* at all than *nouveaux riches*" is not even conceivable here. But it is conceivable in Europe.) Success in business and politics is more visible, and therefore more of a success, in America than success in letters; and while Russians, Germans, and French name their streets after their great writers and poets, Americans are more likely to name them after native vegetation.

The fact is that intellectuals — especially in those intellectual professions in which criteria of excellence are ill-defined — have a problem with the ideal of equality. Their self-esteem and, in many cases, creative energy and

49

raison d'être depend on the inner consciousness and general recognition of their very inequality, superiority to others, the belief that they possess some inherent quality that distinguishes them from and puts them above the rest. In a society based on and dedicated to the premise that all men are created equal, intellectuals are bound to be frustrated and to feel alienated as a result.

Intellectual alienation, indeed, has been a salient feature of American society. It expressed itself, first and foremost, in the myth of the anti-intellectualism of this society, a reflection of its alleged contempt for culture and crass materialism. This myth was born almost as soon as American intellectuals as a group and it could not have been more of a misconception. If now reality resembles the myth, this may be because, as many prophesies born out of frustration, this one was self-fulfilling; but this does not change the fact that when it was conceived, American society, its general population, was better educated and had both more respect and more uses for learning than any of the European societies where intellectuals were held in such enviable (from the point of view of American intellectuals) esteem. Tocqueville wrote in *Democracy in America* that "although America is perhaps in our days the civilized country in which literature is least attended to, still a large number of persons there take an interest in the productions of the mind and make them, if not the study of their lives, at least the charm of their leisure hours. . . . There is hardly a pioneer's hut that does not contain a few odd volumes of Shakespeare. I remember that I read the feudal drama of Henry V for the first time in a log cabin."[10] Nobody, in one's wildest dreams, would imagine "a few odd volumes of Shakespeare" — or Zhukovski, or Racine, or Goethe — among the possessions of Russian, French, or German peasants at the time when he wrote that and decades later, yet Russian, French, and German intellectuals rarely complain about anti-intellectualism of their respective nations. What American intellectuals have found vexing is not being "attended to," not being deferred to as intellectuals, not having the exclusive status of cultural authority, and they did not have this status because, in the United States, culture was not exclusively theirs, it was widely shared.

Since their nation did not grant them the recognition they desired (and the more perfectly it realized its professed ideals, the less likely such recognition became), they did not particularly like their nation. While patriotic effusions by prominent cultural figures are conspicuously — by comparison with other nations — rare in America, its prominent intellectuals have exhibited an equally conspicuous and unparalleled penchant for social criticism — focusing on the shortcomings not just of the government, but of the nation as such.

10. Alexis de Tocqueville, *Democracy in America* (2 vols.), vol. 2, bk. 1, chap. 13; ed. Phillips Bradley (New York: Vintage, 1954), 58.

For a significant number of American intellectuals, the nation's worth was transcended. The nation, in which the status one aspired to could not be attained, had no worth. The solution was to choose a different social framework either through emigration or cosmopolitanism. Intellectual expatriation (specifically, that of writers and artists, though not of scientists) was more characteristic of America than of many countries which supplied America with immigrants. If a French or, more commonly, a German or a Russian writer was frequently an exile, a fugitive from persecution at home, an American intellectual left his home of his own accord, for he found it distasteful. A French, a German, or a Russian writer might not object to being translated, but wherever he lived, his primary audience remained that of his native country; and though he knew that the great majority of his people would never read his works, because they were illiterate or entirely devoid of interest in intellectual matters, he wrote, undaunted by such a state of affairs, for his country. Conversely, an American intellectual, dismayed at the condition of "*true* intellect" in his all-too-literate native land, would not uncommonly be more concerned about "the general interests of the Republic of Letters" than his country, as was Edgar Allan Poe, and, with Poe, "insist upon regarding the world at large as the sole proper audience for the author."[11] Interestingly, in the university system, the status-sensitive intellectuals in America found their "Republic of Letters," an alternative society within the nation, however parochial, where they can legitimately seek and display status based on natural superiority and, as a result, successfully transcend the nation's worth without leaving it or aspiring to world fame.[12]

The most important reason for transcending the nation's worth, underlying the great majority of the attempts to do so, however, is the experience of *national* inferiority. When the worth of the nation was transcended for this reason (that is, when a particular national identity implied indignity, rather than dignity), nationalism in the overwhelming majority of cases

11. Edgar Allan Poe, "Prospectus of the Stylus," in *Essays and Reviews,* ed. G. R. Thompson (New York: Library of America, 1984), 1035. Greenfeld, *Nationalism,* 470.
12. Obviously, I am not implying that these were the sentiments of all American intellectuals — "As so often happens, three options were available to them: loyalty, voice, and exit. They could either accept their society as it was and adjust to whatever approbation and respect they got; try to change their society and make it love them more; or change their frame of reference altogether. The choice of the first option was implicit in the constantly growing number of American scholars and artists. The second was behind much of the rhetoric of American cultural nationalism. The third led to the expatriation or internal exile. Those who chose the two latter options were a minority, but they were highly noticeable, both because they articulated the arguments behind their choice, while the first group — a majority — did not, and because, in the international context, they were unique." (Greenfeld, *Nationalism,* 466.) I also do not wish to imply that status-seeking is the only or the main thing pursued within universities. Obviously, most intellectuals are driven by cultural interests, and universities provide an environment supportive of their pursuit.

was replaced by Marxist socialism or communism. The alternative social framework in this case was the world proletariat.

Marxism, as I have argued,[13] is metamorphosed German nationalism. The inspiration for it, at least in part, was the uncomfortable, the untenable situation of the young Karl Marx, who was a German nationalist (in the sense that he completely agreed with the fundamental tenets of German Romantic nationalism) and a Jew at the same time. A major factor in the formation of German nationalism was the sense of inferiority vis-à-vis and resentment against the West, in Marx's phrasing the "modern" or "advanced nations" of France and England. Owing to the circumstances of its development, German nationalism, from its earliest days in the late eighteenth and the beginning of the nineteenth century, also had strong racist and specifically anti-Semitic connotations. The Jews, though believed an "Asiatic folk," alien to Europe, were seen as the personification of the West and all the evil with which the latter was associated. Excluded from the national communities in which they resided, they were ascribed their own separate nationality (quite independent of their religious affiliation, for, in the eyes of their German compatriots, neither baptism nor atheism affected it). This made being German patriots and sharing in the values of German nationalism psychologically very problematic for the Jews. Marx's theory of history, while keeping intact the underlying ideas of German nationalism (specifically its Manichean vision and its ideas of good and evil with their respective carriers), represented it in the form which solved — or rather eliminated — the Jewish problem. Nations were replaced by classes. National rivalry was economized and represented as class struggle, in general, and in particular as the struggle between the proletariat and Capital. But the incarnation of Capital — the evil in the Marxist scheme — remained the West, and it was the West (with all its riches, power, and especially pretended liberties that made it feel superior to the rest of the world) that was doomed, while the bright future belonged to the proletariat, which whatever else it was, was the anti-West.

The Marxist economization of German nationalism also internationalized it — it became acceptable to national patriots plagued by the sense of inferiority vis-à-vis the West everywhere. This explains why Marxism was so often the program of national movements and why it so well served nationalist interests. This also explains why it has had greatest appeal in societies which had not reached the stage of socioeconomic development when, according to the Marxist theory, the adoption of Marxism would make any sense for them. The reason it was adopted, for example in Russia, had nothing to do with economics and not much more with the alleged

13. "Nationalism and Class Struggle: Two Forces or One?" *Survey: A Journal of East and West Studies* 29 (Autumn 1986): 153–74. See also *Nationalism*.

---

struggle between classes. It had to do, almost exclusively, with one class — the intelligentsia — and its unbearable sense of shame for the nation's (political and moral, much more than economic) backwardness. To be a Russian in the end of the nineteenth century was an embarrassment. One way of dealing with this embarrassment was to dissolve the nation in the economically determined humanity, to transcend the nation for a class or to present it as a class, the spearhead of the international proletariat, which was indeed the gist of Lenin's theory of imperialism.

In certain conditions, socialist internationalism promised more dignity than the nation. The problem was that it transcended the nation's worth while keeping all the characteristics of the nationalisms which were the reasons for such transcendence. Socialism redefined reality and gave the unhappy nationalists new hope of transcending their sense of inferiority and triumphing over the nations they considered superior, but it did not change reality — in fact, it effectively precluded such change — and, as a result, it only perpetuated their resentments, instead of eliminating the grounds for them. It is for this reason that today, with socialism gone, it is nationalism in its old pre-socialist forms, rather than democracy, that takes socialism's place, and that communists *en masse* move to the right-wing nationalist camps.

In Russia this transition (from nationalism camouflaged as internationalism to escape the sense of national inferiority — to nationalism no longer camouflaged because the escape did not work) took seventy years. In other cases it happened quicker. Perhaps the most striking example of an attempted transcendence of the nation's worth for this reason, and then a return to the fold, is that of Benito Mussolini, whose nationalist credentials and exertions need no discussion, but who began as a zealous socialist, more ardently devoted to the idea of the proletarian revolution, we are told, than Rosa Luxemburg or Lenin, a comparison which should speak for itself. His revolutionary ardor was not the only score on which Mussolini compared well with Rosa Luxemburg and Lenin. He, not either of them, could be considered "the first communist in Europe in that he forced the reformists [those who believed the nation the proper framework of socialist activity and insisted on the need to recognize and defer to the national sentiment] out of the party."[14] Mussolini would not recognize the nation, because Italy was not worth recognition. It was backward, poor, and laughable in comparison with its Western neighbors; it commanded no respect, wielded no power, it was much more dignified to be a socialist than to be an Italian. But World War I gave him the hope that Italy could assert itself

14. The discussion of Mussolini relies on Jacob L. Talmon, *Myth of the Nation and Vision of Revolution: Ideological Polarization in the Twentieth Century* (New Brunswick, N.J.: Transaction, 1991).

and take its place among those nations belonging to which brought dignity, and this hope was enough to transform him.

The socialist front of the Russian Empire (alias Soviet Union) to the contrary, few of those who attempted to transcend the worth of the nation with the help of the Marxist doctrine remained faithful to the idea of permanent or world revolution for long. Jews were disproportionately represented among those who did. Marxism appealed to the Jews, among other things, because it promised to deliver them from their nationality, which in those European countries where Marxism had an appeal, such as Germany or Russia, was associated with unbearable indignity. Only in this context can one understand Trotsky's proverbial response to the question "Are you Russian or Jewish?" which was "Neither, I am a socialist." It was embarrassment enough to be a Russian at the time, but Trotsky was not a Russian, and to be a Jew in Russia was plain humiliation. Socialism lifted Jewish Marxists to the dignity of other men, making them equal, and uplifted their spirit. These Jews transcended the worth of the nation, and, unlike their non-Jewish comrades, returned to national identity only because they were forced to do so.

Fluctuations in the worth of the nation have been quite independent of economic trends and changes in technology and communications (the "material infrastructure" of society) to which nationalism has so often been attributed. These fluctuations were related, instead, to the ability of a particular nation to guarantee and safeguard dignified status of its members (whether all, or a specific group) and to the existence of (or belief in) other possibilities for status-enhancement. On the whole, attempts to transcend nationalism have been very rare, both because nationalism usually has been able to satisfy people's need for dignity, and because for the great majority there were not alternative ways to satisfy this need. Economic globalization is unlikely to weaken the grip of nationalism on humanity; it is largely irrelevant to the problem of nationalism. The nation remains worthwhile, even when it is economically (and otherwise) irrational, and if the nation's worth is going to be transcended, it is most improbable that this will be on the account of economic development.

The fact that, from the economic point of view, the world may be turning into a "global village" does not at all contradict this conclusion. Economic globalization is entirely consistent with nationalism. The belief that it spells the end of nationalism is based on the mistaken assumption of the primacy of economics in social life, the idea of economic determinism. But economic cooperation and attempts to promote economic globalization more often than not are seen and undertaken by the participants in the process as means to advance national interests and are not supported if perceived as threatening to the latter. Take for example the European Community (that is, Western European Community, Eastern Europe being at this moment the most convincing proof of the futility of economic considerations when opposed to nationalist passions). It can hardly be interpreted as a sign of nationalism's demise. So long as European unity was limited to economics, the idea aroused no protest and little sentiment in general. But the moment it appeared to threaten national sovereignties and undermine national prestige, the attitude dramatically changed. Now, a substantial proportion of Western Europeans do not want unification, however interdependent their economies. Moreover, it appears that even those who favor it do so for reasons that have little to do with economics and can only be characterized as nationalistic. For example, France, we are told, which is the driving force behind the European Community, sees it as the only hope of remaining a world power. While Mitterrand's "language is European, his interests remain undisguisedly national." He wants to use the European Community "to amplify France's voice on the world stage, and to create strict rules" to counter German influence.[15] As to Germany's reasons for supporting the unification, some fear that it is just trying to "take over the whole of Europe" again. Through a strong federal European Community, they say, Germany could pursue foreign policy without making people suspicious of its nationalistic aspirations.[16]

As to the eventual results of the unification, if it comes through and whatever the intentions of the powers behind it, bringing European nations closer may very well enkindle national sentiments and reignite old resentments, instead of extinguishing them. For it will bring together in one system societies with different levels of international prestige, different levels of cultural achievement and political records, as well as different liv-

15. Alan Riding, "France Pins Hopes on European Unity," *New York Times,* 1 Dec. 1991. France's use of internationalism — and specifically of the European unification — in the interests of French nationalism is not new; one has only to remember that it was Lafayette who, after his sojourn in the United States of America where he aided the cause of independence, on his own testimony, to spite the English, came up with the idea of the United States of Europe — under the leadership of France.
16. Stephen Kinzer, "Germany Now Leading Campaign to Strengthen the European Community," *New York Times,* 2 Dec. 1991. One could, of course, bring examples from this hemisphere as well. For example, Robert Reich, in his famous book *The Work of Nations* (1991), believes economic globalization to be a good reason to reconsider and redefine American *national* interests and an opportunity to reorient national — patriotic — energies. (It is significant that the epigraph of the book is a quotation from Calvin Coolidge: "Patriotism is easy to understand. . . . It means looking out for yourself by looking out for your country.") Many American business leaders and authors on business view open-borders trade agreements and multinational corporations as the means to advance American national interests in the conditions of global economy; see *The Global Marketplace,* ed. J. M. Rosow, (New York: Facts on File, 1988). Nationalism seems to favor economic internationalism in certain conditions. In a way, this is no different from Lenin's advocacy of ideological internationalism as a foundation of the national pride of the Great Russians ("O nazional'noi gordosti velikorossov," 1914). On the other hand, others openly advocate mercantilism, and it is possible that these are the majority; see Robert Kutner, *The End of Laissez-Faire* (New York: Alfred A. Knopf, 1991).

ing standards — every variety of the haves and the have-nots — and this will create a fertile ground for envy. Envy has been a most potent inspiration for virulent, dangerous nationalism. The European Community thus may give new life to the monster it is believed to have buried. It should be remembered that nationalism originally was able to spread only because a degree of globalization already existed (it is no accident that it first spread in Europe, united as it was by ties of religion, common culture, *and trade*).

I believe that the nation's worth is not about to be transcended as yet. But I also believe in the infinite creativity of the human mind, and I believe that out of our discontent may be born a better means to satisfy our desire for respect, which would make possible a better world, as nationalism was born out of the discontent of the sixteenth-century nobles, who made our world possible. As long as history goes on, there is hope.

Nationalism, Internationalism, and Economics

Peter M. Oppenheimer

T HIS PAPER falls into three distinct sections. The first briefly out-
lines the market economist's view of the state. The second explains
the involvement of economists with national policy-making and
its relation to their professional standing. The final section considers how
far the character of economic policy-making is affected by contemporary
emphasis on interdependence and economic integration.

The Economist's Focus

Economists are interested in the state as a policy-making and institution-
creating body. They ask what economic functions the state should perform,
and in their answers try to take account of the economic forces confronting
it, including those arising from international trade and finance. They
acknowledge, indeed emphasize, that differences in constitutional structure (unitary, federal, confederal . . .) may alter the way in which state economic responsibilities are fulfilled. And they note that sovereignty is not
indivisible across subject areas. The European Community, for instance,
was initially a customs union, so the Commission in Brussels has been
given responsibility for determining commercial policy vis-à-vis non-
member countries, even though there has so far been little or no unified
European policy in other domains.[1]

In their professional capacity economists have only a secondary and indirect interest in questions of cultural or ethnic identity which may concern

---

1. Actually the Commission's powers are only partial, and indeed the customs union itself has
to this day remained incomplete. In particular, France and Italy have maintained national quotas on imports from Japan of automobiles and consumer electronics. The future phaseout of
these quotas is still (1992) not totally assured. One other point: the Common Agricultural
Policy is correctly viewed as an aspect of the customs union, since creation of the latter
involved unifying agricultural protection across member countries.

other investigators. Whether the spread of multinational corporations diminishes the scope for macroeconomic management by national governments is an important question for economists. But whether international migration is gradually turning national societies into multicultural ones is of little concern. It acquires interest only if economic structures are affected. For example, the growth of the (ethnically) Asian populations in Britain has helped to influence the country's pattern of retail trade. The fact that Asian-owned corner shops are open for business until eight or ten o'clock in the evening and on Sundays has been one factor causing national food supermarket chains to do the same. (Other factors include rising labor-force participation among women, which makes daytime shopping more difficult.)

In short, economists are concerned with the state rather than with the nation, with the domain of legal and political authority rather than with cultural or linguistic personality.

The reason is straightforward. What economists want from the collectivity is a set of arrangements to permit and encourage the optimum functioning of markets. The Smithian minimum is a system of law and order, of property rights and of the sanctity of contracts — together with external defense. These are the classic "collective goods," whose consumption is both non-exclusive to individuals and non-confinable to any specified subgroup of citizens, and which are therefore not satisfactorily provided by individualistic markets. Economists will also be keen to monitor the *costs* of government and of the legal system, to see whether the citizen is getting value for money.

Beyond the Smithian minimum, nearly all economists see some further role for the state in areas not satisfactorily managed by market forces alone, though what these areas are soon becomes a matter of dispute. Old-fashioned liberals (in the British sense) will stress the need to curb monopolies and restrictive practices. Newfangled liberals (in the American sense) will wish to see redistributive taxation and/or public welfare services to mitigate the inequalities of wealth and income commonly thrown up by market systems. The mitigation of (at any rate extreme) fluctuations in economic activity and employment is generally agreed to be a task for governments and central banks, though there are disagreements about method (mainly concerning the amount of discretion as against rule-bound behavior which the authorities should permit themselves). Other agenda items include activities with significant "externalities" (spillovers) — both beneficial ones to be encouraged (such as scientific research) and harmful ones to be curbed (such as pollution).

At this juncture, there is no reason for the economist to be wedded to any particular form or level of governmental organization — except that which is judged to be most cost-effective for the purpose at hand; and this will vary with circumstances. Policies to reduce transfrontier pollution may require either a supranational authority or cooperation between national authorities, but there are no *a priori* grounds for preferring one to the other. Policies for reducing unemployment in a single country appropriate when others are enjoying a boom may be rightly criticized as "beggar-my-neighbor" when unemployment is a near-universal problem.

The chances of government action succeeding in its objectives also vary greatly from issue to issue. Regulations to diminish air pollution by motor vehicles are usually enforceable with little trouble. Policies to mitigate income inequalities are, by contrast, somewhat hit-and-miss. Intuition suggests that they become more hit-and-miss the larger the population being considered[2] — but, of course, the smaller the population over which they are applied, the more likely it is that objectionable inequalities will fall outside the policy mechanism altogether.

In important domains the likelihood of government policy succeeding will be enhanced if it is based on a wide-ranging consensus of the population. Since 1945 this has applied, for instance, to Germany's emphasis on price stability, or to Sweden's welfare state and manpower training facilities. Consensus is presumably easier to achieve the more homogeneous the population and the more that popular attitudes are determined by shared historical memories. To that extent the economist may entertain a legitimate bias in favor of the nation-state rather than anything bigger.

Such bias, however, is tempered by cosmopolitanism. This term does not signify a leaning towards world or even continental government. I know of no evidence that the per capita resource costs of good government and good legal systems decrease with economic size. (If one looks at the number and remuneration of lawyers in the United States compared with a typical European country, one is tempted to conclude precisely the opposite.) In a few respects global institutions are theoretically optimal: a single world economy would obviate the costs of international money currency and the inconvenience of price translation. But these are trivial considerations beside the mass of structural, cultural, and psychological factors which make political boundaries unavoidable. The point is rather that such boundaries should (like transport costs) obstruct the global division of labor no more than is minimally necessary. Consumers should have access both to the cheapest sources of particular goods and services and to the widest possible variety (international trade in differentiated consumer products being a conspicuous feature of modern economies). Borrowing and lending — that is, inter-temporal trade — should likewise be conducted in a global marketplace. Technology should be internationally diffused.

---

2. At a global level, as we all know, foreign aid is a mechanism for transferring money from poor people in rich countries to rich people in poor countries.

Peter M. Oppenheimer

Economics in the Service of National Objectives

Equipped with the foregoing combination of professional attitudes, economists are well placed to contribute, in their desiccated fashion, to what Senator Moynihan has called the containment of collective egoism. But, like their own explanatory models, economists are also liable to fall short of their theoretical potential when it comes to practical application. In this section of the paper I try to explain why, with the help of illustrations from economic theory and from some recent issues of policy.

In a word, economists are liable, often against their own better judgment, to be drawn into — or seduced by — a nationalistic approach to policy questions. This is for two reasons. First, economists seek to act as technical advisors, not as policymakers in their own right. (It is unnecessary for present purposes to be cynical about this claim.) They are therefore bound to develop a working relationship with those currently in charge of policy, and to apply their professional techniques to devising and defending measures congenial to their political masters.[3] Admittedly, they may also do their best to dissuade politicians from actions which seem economically misguided; but if that is all they do, they are unlikely to last long as advisors. Moreover, politicians for their part will at times wish to respond to constituency demands, and require their economic advisors to investigate possible rationales for popular measures, notably those giving protection or subsidization to interests which can be presented as in some way national.

Secondly, the application of economics to practical issues frequently involves judgment between competing arguments or items of evidence. Clear-cut theorems or quasi-scientific results nearly always depend on specific assumptions whose relevance to the real world can be debated: Is this or is this not a case where market failure justifies certain types of government intervention? How likely is it that inflation expectations will be permanently worsened if a further depreciation of the exchange rate leads to an increase in this year's inflation from 3.5 percent to 4.8 percent? And so on. In short, the intellectual characteristics of economics as a discipline allow it within broadish limits to be bent in defense of politically preferred courses of action.

Nowhere are these points more vividly illustrated than in the field of international trade and protectionism. The case for free trade is part and parcel of the case for free markets in general. There is a long and complex history here, going back well over two centuries. Early chapters include the arguments of Hume and Adam Smith against simple mercantilism — or bullionism, as one should more accurately call it — and Ricardo's formulation of the principle of comparative advantage to attack the British Corn

3. Edmund Dell puts the point less politely, describing economists as the "running dogs" of politicians. See Edmund Dell, "The Wistful Liberalism of Deepak Lal," *The World Economy* 2 (May 1979): 189.

Laws. Over the years economists have refined and formalized the logic underlying the market system. A lot of attention has been given to "market failure" and possible remedies for it, i.e., cases where market mechanisms left to themselves may fail to deliver an optimum allocation of resources. The Smithian collective goods mentioned in section one are a prime example. Arguments for trade intervention such as tariffs stem from other kinds of market failure, real or alleged. The intellectual impulse to extend the analytical frontiers of economics has been intertwined with political motives such as the urge to support particular government strategies.

The common feature of all economic arguments for tariffs is a focus on the national economic interest. In the political domain governments are susceptible to demands for protection against global competition from sectional producer interests (farmers, textile firms, computer manufacturers). Such interests are able because of their concentration (both geographically and in producer organizations) to influence the political process. Consumers or taxpayers who bear the costs of protection may not be aware of these, and even if they are, cannot usually assemble a countervailing lobby because of their diffuseness. The hallmark of the economist as against the politician is to rule out any case for interference with international trade which cannot be shown at least *prima facie* to be in the national rather than in a purely sectional interest.

Arguments for tariffs which have this property and hence occasion respectable debate within the economics profession fall mostly into three categories. One, comprising so-called infant industry arguments, is concerned with the capacity of markets to facilitate industrial development and structural change. A second is concerned with the exploitation of monopolies. The third views tariffs as an instrument of stabilization policy, i.e., as helping to maintain high employment and stable prices combined with a sustainable trade balance (or balance of payments on current account).

Infant-industry arguments for tariff protection go back at least to Friedrich List in the early nineteenth century. Their general tenor was that free trade hampered the transformation of poor countries or backward sectors by locking them into existing lines of (mostly primary) production; the way to develop, therefore, was to industrialize by engaging in import-substitution behind tariff or other import barriers. This line of thinking gave way round about 1970 to the philosophy of "outward looking," export-led industrialization which is now part of the World Bank's orthodoxy. The change was due partly to the dismal experiences of a number of countries (notably in Latin America) which followed the import-substitution route, by contrast with the startling success of early practitioners of the outward-looking approach, mainly the Southeast Asian "tigers." But it also owed a great deal to theoretical advances, including the demonstration (pioneered by H. G. Johnson) that most of the shortcomings of markets cited from time to time as theoretical arguments for trade intervention turn out on closer inspection to be mainly arguments for intervention in *domestic* markets, including capital markets and markets for education and training, leaving free trade intact.[4]

The other two categories of argument likewise have a long history. As regards monopoly, the so-called "optimum tariff" argument, or terms of trade argument for tariffs, goes back at least to J. S. Mill. The essence of this argument is that where a country has some monopoly or monopsony power in world markets—i.e., is large enough in either its export or its import markets to influence the world-market price of these products—then it can in principle achieve a net gain in real income by restricting its willingness to trade, thereby causing a rise in the price of its exports and/or a fall in the price of imports. The gain from this price change can be shown to outweigh the simultaneous loss due to the shrinkage of trade volumes and associated diminution of international specialization. The net gain to the tariff-imposing country must, however, be smaller than the loss to the rest of the world, since both parties lose from the restriction of trade volumes whereas the price effect is a zero-sum game—one party's plus matches the other's minus. The theorem also assumes that the "victim" countries do not (or cannot) retaliate. Subject to these provisos the argument is theoretically watertight. In practice, it is doubtful whether conditions for a lasting and successful application of this theorem by any single country have ever been identified.[5]

4. Other major analytical contributions came from (i) the theory of effective protection (elaborated by W. M. Corden, Bela Balassa, and others), which revealed the enormously high level of protection accorded to some industrial producers in less developed countries; (ii) the demonstration by I. M. D. Little and others of the value of using world-market prices as benchmarks of opportunity cost in a development context; and (iii) the theory of rent-seeking (pioneered by Anne Krueger), which called attention to previously neglected forms of resource misallocation engendered by protectionist policies. As often happens, the "outward-looking" orthodoxy has perhaps gone too far in downgrading the role of the state altogether. Paul R. Krugman has recently suggested that some aspects of the earlier school of development economics deserve revival, notably their emphasis on economies of scale, external economies (through labor training and the diffusion of technology), and "strategic complementarity" of various industrial sectors. This line of argument, however, in no way rehabilitates the case for intervention in import or export markets—the distinction between external and domestic market intervention having not been highlighted in the literature of the 1940s and 1950s. See Paul R. Krugman, "Towards a Counter-Counter Revolution in Development Theory," in *World Bank Annual Conference on Development Economics,* ed. Laurence H. Summers and Shekhar Shah (Washington, D.C.: International Bank for Reconstruction and Development—The World Bank, 1993), 15–38. Among the seminal works cited by Krugman is Paul Rosenstein-Rodan's "Problems of Industrialization of Eastern and South-Eastern Europe," a paper whose geographic focus alone must arouse interest in the 1990s (*Economic Journal* 53 [1943]: 202–11).

5. In this context I must cite the passing comment by Paul R. Krugman in his editorial introduction to the widely cited conference volume *Strategic Trade Policy and the New International Economics:* "Nobody would suggest that Saudi Arabia would be richer with free trade" (Cam-

Nonetheless, in the United States proposals for import tariffs, possibly combined with either export subsidies or production subsidies (the latter strictly not a trade measure) have in the past decade attracted significant support, both political and academic, on all three grounds specified in our classification of arguments: industrial modernization, monopoly rent-shifting, and external payments equilibrium. The support has arisen from a sense of dissatisfaction with U.S. economic performance, notably the external payments deficit, near-zero growth of labor productivity, and allegedly waning industrial competitiveness in hi-tech sectors such as electronics.

Support for protectionism has, of course, been patchy and intermittent. It has also rested on various types of special pleading, and the neglect of relatively obvious explanations of U.S. macroeconomic trends. The external payments deficit has been associated with a more or less parallel deficit in the U.S. budget position — the "twin deficits." The association is not a coincidence. The government sector has been borrowing, year in and year out, sums larger than the U.S. private sector has had available to lend; the limited availability of U.S. private funds has reflected the low level of U.S. private (household plus corporate) savings, the bulk of which are absorbed by U.S. private capital formation. The excess of government borrowing over U.S. private-sector net lending was bound to be met by borrowing from overseas, whose counterpart is the deficit on current account.

A feature of the U.S. situation is that the external deficit has not been radically affected by exchange-rate movements. The 40-percent depreciation of the dollar in 1985–87 from its overvalued peak in February 1985 gave a substantial boost to U.S. exports and prolonged the cyclical upswing into 1989. But there was little improvement in either the current account deficit or the federal budget position, because imports responded sharply to the rise in domestic output, but tax revenue did not. This combination of events does not reflect any iron law of economics. It so happens, however, that if U.S. private savings behavior retains its recent pattern, elimination of the current payments deficit will depend on policy action to narrow the government budget deficit, while movements of the dollar exchange rate have their main impact on the level of national output.

The overvaluation of the dollar in 1984–85 generated a serious profits squeeze in the tradable goods sectors of the U.S. economy, and an upsurge

bridge: MIT Press, 1986; ed. Paul R. Krugman), 11. Offhand illustrations are a dangerous thing. A strong case can be made that Saudi Arabia would indeed be (or would have been) better off with free trade in any but the shortest time horizon. When Krugman was writing (presumably 1985, a few months after the conference in late October 1984) he evidently had not bothered to observe events on the world oil market. The Saudis were then on the verge of triggering a collapse of world oil prices precisely because their previous policy of restricting exports in order to keep the price up was seen as benefiting not themselves but only their OPEC partners (and non-OPEC oil producers) who declined to match Saudi restraint.

Peter M. Oppenheimer

in sectional demands for protectionist measures. This was assuaged by the exchange-rate and export developments of 1985–89, but not eliminated. The continuing current-account deficit, stagnant labor productivity, and the conspicuous rise in Japanese direct investment in the United States have fostered resentment against supposedly "unfair" competition from foreign, chiefly Japanese, producers.[6]

One reflection of this is the aggressive "Super 301" clause in the 1989 U.S. Trade Act, authorizing the imposition of discriminatory trade barriers against countries identified as running excessive bilateral trade surpluses with the United States. Another is the meticulous scholarly search since the early 1980s for arguments which might justify "strategic" protection or subsidization for hi-tech U.S. industries threatened by Japanese competition. The search includes empirical analyses of "how the Japanese did it" (and especially whether government promotion played a significant role) as well as models of strategic interaction among oligopolistic firms.[7]

The focus of the theoretical analyses is on two features supposedly both associated with expansion of knowledge-intensive industries: external economies (spillovers) and economic rent (i.e., elements of monopoly income, linked in this case with patents or simply with being one jump ahead of competitors in the marketplace). The rigor and sophistication of the theoretical contributions is not in question. But as possible guides to policy they are no more appealing than the old theorem on optimum tariffs. Indeed, the suggestion that government policies may be used to appropriate a larger share of the rent available from global markets is similar in type to an optimum tariff argument, the difference being chiefly that it relies on reducing the market share of foreign suppliers rather than on reducing the price of their products.

The change is, in my opinion, a weakness: first, because "strategic" protection, unlike optimum tariffs on a commodity, depends ultimately on the government "picking winners" among domestic firms; and secondly, because the extent of rent available to be extracted from information-intensive industries is far from evident. The sector is highly competitive and long-run profitability insecure, even for leading players (e.g., IBM). The sector with the most conspicuous prospects for market pricing above the opportunity-cost of production and hence obtaining rent is not computers and electronics but oil and gas (albeit largely excluding the United

6. A frequently cited non-Japanese example of "strategic" industrial assistance is that of the European Airbus. This aircraft did indeed benefit from government financial backing. Even so, its producers remain financially weak; and but for it, U.S. producers would have a near-total dominance of large-airliner markets outside the former Communist bloc. Whatever else this example shows, it does not testify to U.S. competitive weakness.

7. Besides the volume cited in footnote 5, a collection of somewhat more technical papers is *Monopolistic Competition and International Trade,* ed. H. Kierzkowski (Oxford: Clarendon Press, 1984). The seminal paper is by James Brander and Barbara Spencer, "Tariff Protection and Imperfect Competition," 194–206.

64

States' own production). The U.S. administration should begin the attack on its twin deficits with a hefty excise on gasoline, rather than by seeking to protect U.S. manufacturers from the will-o'-the-wisp of "unfair Japanese advantage."[8]

Interdependence and Integration

If the intensification of international economic relations brings benefits (which it does), it also brings greater interdependence. Countries become less constrained by domestic resource availabilities, and more constrained by the behavior of trading partners and of foreign governments. They become less vulnerable to domestic economic disasters (such as crop failures) and more exposed to shocks from abroad (such as sharp movements in the oil price).

Today's economic interdependence is not as unprecedented as many commentators like to imply. As far as can be made out, the ratio of foreign trade to GNP in leading countries in the generation before 1914 was not very different from the figures recorded in the 1970s and 1980s.[9] Britain's foreign investment before 1914 — an important engine of growth for the rest of the world — gives rise to a particularly striking example. By 1913 the total value of Britain's overseas assets, much of it in the form of fixed-interest (bond) holdings, had reached an estimated £4 billion, a little short of $20 billion (at £1 = $4.86). To convert this into, say, its 1980 equivalent, one may multiply by an index of United States money GNP, which on the basis of 1913 = 1 is approximately 20. Thus one comes up with a figure of about $400 billion for the 1980 equivalent. This, as it happens, is the rough total of external assets held at that date by OPEC countries.

Britain's overseas asset buildup before 1913 was spread over several decades and took place mostly through the non-bank capital market in which individual savers placed their funds. The OPEC states accumulated

8. The frequent use of the epithet in U.S. discussions of this issue calls to mind the attitude of John de Stogumber in G. B. Shaw's *St. Joan,* scene 4: "We were not fairly beaten, my Lord. No Englishman is ever fairly beaten."
9. The following data for Britain are taken from R. C. O. Matthews, C. H. Feinstein, and J. C. Odling-Smee, *British Economic Growth 1856–1973* (London: Oxford University Press, 1982), 432–33:

UK Import and Export Ratios
(at current prices)

Year	Ratio of Imports of Goods to GNP	Ratio of Exports to GDP	
		Goods	Goods and Services
1873	24.5%	21.0%	28.5%
1913	25.9	22.5	30.1
1973	23.0	18.1	26.1

much of their overseas wealth in less than a decade (after the oil price rise of 1973–74), largely through the international commercial banking system. Serious stability problems ensued with the onset of the Third-World debt crisis in 1982. By contrast, before 1913 defaults (admittedly less extensive) caused loss to individual bondholders but did not threaten the stability of financial institutions. The contrast, however, lies in the nature of institutional arrangements, not in the degree of world financial integration. Admittedly, focus on OPEC external claims and LDC debts leaves out the role of multinational corporations and the huge post-1950 volume of direct international investments (especially by U.S. companies, and latterly Japanese).

If one turns to Europe, the ambitions of the EC — following the Single European Act (1985), the Delors Report (1989), and the negotiation of the Maastricht Treaty (1991) — to intensify the unification of the European economy and in particular to establish a single currency represent in basic respects a wish to return to the pre-1914 situation. There were, at that time, no formal obstacles to the movement of capital or labor across Europe. To be sure, systems of company and commercial law were not unified; but then, there was much less company and commercial law to unify — not to speak of financial regulation which was almost wholly informal and self-imposed. Travel (except to Russia) required no passport. There was effective monetary union, as countries were on the gold standard and exchange rates were regarded as immutable. There were, interestingly, national import tariffs, most conspicuously in Germany, on both manufactures and foodstuffs. Yet, given the much smaller role of government finances in the economy generally, these tariffs were arguably of no greater significance than today's differences in national rates of indirect taxation (VAT and excise duty) as infringements of the single market principle.

Altogether, the conspicuous difference between pre-1914 and nowadays lies not in the degree of economic interdependence but in the economic role of government, which has expanded to an extent that Victorian and Edwardian citizens would find breathtaking.

The ratio of public-sector spending to GNP in west European countries, estimated typically at 10–15 percent before 1914, has been mostly between 40 and 50 percent since 1970 (significantly higher, incidentally, than in the United States and Japan, where the figure is nearer 30 percent).[10] The secular increase in all these percentages is due principally to the rise in state-financed social security and public services (especially education and in some cases health). Grants and subsidies to transport and other industrial sectors have also been significant, as has military spending.

10. The figure is unaffected by privatization of nationalized industries such as occurred in Britain in the 1980s. This reduces the public sector's share of national *output* but not that of expenditure.

Increased public spending accompanied acceptance after World War II in all advanced countries of government responsibility for (something like) full employment—the two changes stemming from common political and intellectual roots, even if not linked by logical necessity. In addition, governments have been drawn into enacting and enforcing regulations over wide areas of economic life, ranging from advertising standards through environmental cleanliness and safety to financial-market behavior and corporate governance.

This vast enlargement of the economic scope and expectations of government has been maintained regardless of the professed political philosophy of incumbent politicians. President Reagan and Mrs. Thatcher in the 1980s did not significantly "roll back the frontiers of the state." They did not even disclaim responsibility for aggregate employment, even though they repudiated (insofar as they understood) the Keynesian macroeconomics on which the post-1945 full-employment commitment had been based. They maintained merely that the route to full employment lay through stable prices, a flexible labor market, and cuts in direct personal tax rates. What is striking is not how much but how little the economic role of government has been constrained by today's economic interdependence between countries.

The point sheds light on some prominent aspects of today's internationalism in general and of the European Community in particular. *It accounts in fact for much of the contemporary emphasis on international economic cooperation.* Initially, the main international economic organizations (the IMF, GATT, and the OEEC) were set up to facilitate reconstruction after World War II in the light of inter-war experience and the Keynesian revolution in economics. Subsequently, the machinery of cooperation has been increasingly employed by governments to try to shift policy dilemmas onto others, or at least to share them. Sometimes negotiations have been necessitated by a clash of regulatory or fiscal interests. The U.S. authorities (at either the federal or state level) have periodically sought to extend their legislative or regulatory reach into other jurisdictions, by seeking to exercise control both over foreign branches or subsidiaries of U.S. firms and over foreign firms with affiliates or subsidiaries in the United States. It is one-sided and indeed misleading to describe such situations in terms of multinational business limiting the scope for national fiscal policies or other types of economic management. The limits arise from the conflicting national interests of countries and/or from underlying economic scarcities and opportunity costs. Multinational corporations are not an additional obstacle. They are merely an institutional channel through which the underlying factors operate—operate perhaps more swiftly and sensitively (this much may be conceded) than might otherwise have been the case.

It is acknowledged that public regulations in the fields of health, safety, consumer protection and elsewhere can act, intentionally or otherwise, as non-tariff barriers to trade. The issue received considerable attention in the Tokyo Round of GATT negotiations in the 1970s. Within the European Community it provides a rationale for the Commission to assert itself and to seek centralization and harmonization of regulations across the Community. Following the celebrated "cassis de Dijon" case in the early 1980s,[11] Commissioner Cockfield succeeded in selling the idea of "mutual recognition" as a substitute for harmonization in the Single European Act (1984) and subsequent drive to complete the single market.

The last point is subtler than appears at first sight. Must there, for example, be a single pan-European scheme of company law? Or a ban on national tax discrimination in the sphere of household saving?[12] Company law is not fully uniform across the United States. It is well known that corporations have found registration in the state of Delaware attractive as a means of discouraging hostile takeover bids. Similarly, household tax systems vary from state to state in the U.S.A. and from canton to canton in Switzerland, which also has four official languages. Yet the United States and Switzerland are each considered on any practical criterion to constitute a single market. What appears to be necessary for the perception of a single market is a sufficient weight of common laws, institutions, habits, and culture within which diversity on other matters can be accommodated. There is no fixed list of what has to be common. The problem in the EC is that irretrievable diversity on so many matters is so great that uniformity has to be striven for whenever possible if the psychology of the single market is ever to take root.

While the EC Commission acts as a lobby for harmonization, politicians promoting the construction and development of the EC are pursuing essentially nationalistic objectives on two levels. The first level is that of existing nation-states. The French, most obviously, treat the EC as a vehicle for the enhancement of France's global status and influence. In the immediate European context this means basically seeking leverage over the Federal Republic, if possible by controlling what German policymakers and corporate decision-makers do in the external domain, and otherwise by contradicting or upstaging German actions and so in some measure neutralizing them. A striking example was France's joining in the Gulf War

11. In this case the European Court held, in effect, that beverages whose constituents were approved under French law could not be excluded from the German market on the grounds that they would not have been approved under German law.

12. The Community has hitherto remained permissive towards national tax discrimination in favor of local financial institutions. For example, tax deductibility of life insurance premiums may be limited to cases where the insurance company is of the same nationality as the taxing authority. See David R. F. Simpson, "Unfinished Business of the Single Market," in *Finance and the International Economy 6,* ed. R. O'Brien (Oxford: The Amex Bank Review Prize Essays, 1992), 137–44.

against Saddam Hussein in 1991, when Germany pleaded a constitutional bar on its own participation. The fact that the dominant role of the United States in this war was *ad hoc* and not based on NATO probably also facilitated the French decision. A more trivial instance was President Mitterrand's visit to beleaguered communities in ex-Yugoslavia in 1992, some months after Germany's decision to recognize Croatia as an independent state forced the hand of the European Community as a whole — itself a nice example of national politics determining EC decisions.

A different kind of national-state interest is that of the Italians. Both policymakers and public opinion in Italy appear to view EC membership as a means of forcing overdue improvements in their own national machinery of government and public administration. The Banca d'Italia, having long struggled to contain inflation in Italy, is a strong advocate of a European Monetary Union in which the task of price stabilization will be handed over to a wider forum molded in large part by the German Bundesbank. The 1992 upheaval in the European Monetary System represents a setback to these ambitions, but has not altered the ultimate objective. Many other Italians welcome the prospect of subordinating politicians in Rome to the authorities in Brussels, on the grounds that the latter are less corrupt (probable but not certain) and will make government in Italy both more efficient and less colored by the country's North-South divide.

More briefly on some other EC members, the lower-income countries (Greece, Ireland, Portugal, Spain) have the vested interest of receiving sizeable transfers from their wealthier EC partners. By contrast, the interest of the Federal Republic in a further strengthening of European institutions has basically diminished in recent years, first because of reunification and secondly because of the growing realization that monetary union in Europe would to some extent undermine the power of the Bundesbank (or its successor) to pursue the goal of price stability within the Federal Republic.

The second level of nationalistic objectives in Europe is the level of the EC itself. Neither the Community's intellectual origins nor its current *raison d'être* is economic. Jean Monnet and the founding fathers were concerned (like Chamberlain and Pétain) to provide a lasting basis for peace in Western Europe. The Community's goal today is to enlarge Europe's role and influence in world affairs. Achievements in this respect have so far been unimpressive, focusing almost exclusively on commercial policy and including periodic quarrels with the United States and other agricultural exporters over aspects of the Common Agricultural Policy, in which the Community has been basically in the wrong and the rest of the world basically in the right.

The Israeli Prime Minister (Mr. Rabin) scored at least a debating point in 1992 when he asked how the EC could feel entitled to demand a role in the Middle East peace process when it was incapable of acting to halt internecine strife in Yugoslavia.[13]

Closer to home, a further widening of EC membership to include Austria, Finland, and Sweden is likely during the 1990s. But the Community has still to develop a coherent approach to its relations with former COMECON countries, as well as to the implications of successive enlargements for its internal structure and institutions. Whether development of a common EC foreign and defense policy is compatible even with the existing Community of twelve is highly doubtful, and with a larger Community still more doubtful. The difficulty lies not in the number of sovereign units but in the diversity of their objectives and attitudes in world affairs. On present prospects the geopolitical status of the EC is unlikely to advance beyond that of a loosely and periodically cooperating alliance of nation-states.

The fact that international cooperation in a variety of forms is one (or several) of the channels through which governments pursue national objectives is hardly startling news. And cooperation is obviously better than trade wars or other forms of policy designed to discriminate against foreigners. But one must not be misled by this, or by the fact that European countries are trying to create some new form of confederal political organization, into supposing that the nation-state is an anachronism in economic affairs.

13. Mr. Rabin doubtless had also not forgotten the Venice Declaration of 1980, one of the few attempts by EC governments acting in unison to claim a role for the EC in international affairs, in this case Israeli-Arab relations. The Declaration was seen by the Israelis not merely as biased against them but, more important, as prejudging the outcome of matters which required negotiation (viz., recognition of Palestinian political rights).

Olympianism and the Denigration of Nationality

Kenneth R. Minogue

Olympianism as a New Universalism

TO UNDERSTAND why the worth of nations has recently become a subject of denigration, we must take our bearings from the conflict between the rationalism of the Enlightenment and the nationalism of the romantic period. The beginnings of this conflict may be dated from the end of the eighteenth century, and its most profound statement is no doubt that provided by Hegel's reflections on the theme of universal and particular. His *Philosophy of Right* is a brilliant attempt to integrate these two components of our understanding into a coherent whole.

In the politics of recent centuries, however, one emphasis or other has dominated human striving. In the universalist tradition, many have dreamed of a new world order specified in terms of nature and rights, culminating perhaps in a world government. Others, following Herder and bewitched by particularity, have sought salvation in a return to local cultural roots. Some ideas, such as community, have become a battleground between these two human tendencies: Marx's conception of a classless community represents universalism in its most uncompromising form, but nationalists like Mazzini have thought that a real human community could only be constructed out of the particularity of primary national loyalties.

These, of course, have been the enthusiasms of intellectuals who live by ideas; but even in the practices of liberal democratic societies, we may observe the dialectical dance of universal and particular. It is especially conspicuous in times of high conflict, as in war. Generally, one theme is dominant, the other recessive, and it is a situation of this kind which I propose to analyze.

Kenneth R. Minogue

Communism being dead, most forms of contemporary universalism have come to focus on a supposed moral superiority in international institutions over the sovereignty of national states. In some contexts, people moved by such a judgment are called "cosmopolitans," a term which brings out a common feature of such an international allegiance, namely, a rejection of local affections and allegiances. This rejection may in some cases amount to a form of national self-hatred of the kind that, by way of the Marxist version of universalism, led many inhabitants of the twentieth century to become the "political pilgrims" of some adoptive patriotism — the Soviet Union, China, Cuba, Albania, and the like. Such self-hatred, in which the individual rejects his own community, commonly involves a certain contempt for the majority of people who have not.

Such an attitude of detachment might suitably be called "Olympianism."[1] The essential allegiance of the Olympian is to those who share his belief wherever they may be, in contradistinction to fellow nationals. It will be clear that one has only to set up the most elementary specification of this faith in international institutions to discover that the basic ideological distinction between elite and mass, the few who have discovered the true situation and the many still lost in outdated passions and ideas, locks easily into place. Olympianism trades on old habits of thought.

The strength of Olympianism in our century owes much to reflection upon two world wars in which national and ideological loyalties led to death and destruction. The lesson learned by many was that nationalism was the basic cause of large-scale human conflict, and that its consequences were so dreadful as to render the very concept of national sovereignty a dangerous anachronism. Nation-states were, in the view of the theologian Reinhold Niebuhr, forms of collective egoism.[2] The path of virtue must therefore lie in redirecting human loyalties away from collective aggression towards international cooperation. A utopia of managed perfection could be glimpsed by the educated Olympian as a distant horizon to which we must travel, the true object of loyalty for those capable of transcending the pull of national allegiance.

Mistakes About Nationalism

Olympianism is the doctrine which has generated the popular idea that nationalism lies at the root of all conflict in the world. And it is worth looking at this particular belief in some detail because doctrines no less than people are revealed by the mistakes they make.

1. I owe this term to John O'Sullivan, who adopted it from a remark by the historian Macauley: "An acre in Middlesex," he wrote in an essay on Lord Bacon in the *Edinburgh Review* of 1837, "is better than a principality in Utopia." "Utopianism," however, is a term referring to things much broader than I am concerned with here. Hence — Olympianism.
2. *Moral Man and Immoral Society: A Study in Ethics and Politics* (London: Charles Scribner's Sons, 1932).

The first error is that nationalism may be found as far back as the historical record stretches. Wherever states have been pitted against each other, the cause of conflict lies in the national identification which holds each side together. The Hundred Years' War between the English and the French in the late Middle Ages, for example, has often been taken as a nationalist conflict. Scholarly opinion now recognizes, however, that nationalism is a doctrine invented at the end of the eighteenth century.[3] It is the belief that conflict is basically caused by foreign rule, alias imperialism, and that every nation must have its own state. This view is, I say, pretty widely recognized, but not beyond the possibility of recidivism. A recent writer persuaded of its truth, however, may stand as an example of how easy it is to reinstate the error: Eric Hobsbawm agrees that nationalism is historically recent, but can still talk of a political form which he calls "proto-nationalism" and discovers as far back as the eleventh century.[4] What lies behind this mistake is a confusion between the *idea* of nationalism on the one hand, and any aggressive cultural loyalty on the other. "Us" against "them" is no doubt an old story; nationalism is a new pretext.

A related error blames the disasters of this century on nationalist doctrine. In fact, however, the First World War emerged from a breakdown of the balance of power and the imperial, not nationalist, ambitions of Germany. The Second World War was ideologically inspired by Nazism, a universalist doctrine based not on the nation but on the superiority of the Aryan race. Genuine German patriotism (as the 1944 plot suggests) was notably hostile to Hitler.

These mistakes are commonly linked to a wider doctrine which analyzes the modern world in terms of increasing global interdependence. The national sovereignty of modern states is in this analysis first identified with an unreal omnipotence and then pronounced an anachronism. The Olympian posture here is that of a farsighted figure recognizing what in one version is called "the politics of interdependence" and drawing appropriate conclusions from it.[5] We are living in a period of transition to a new epoch, and internationalism is keeping up with the new times, recognizing that no state alone these days can resist the perils threatening the environment or the speculations of bankers.

It is a familiar device of rhetoric to advance the currency of an idea by presenting it as a new and brilliant solution to a problem which has only just been detected. Human life has always, however, been highly vulnerable to what was going on abroad, and recent increases in global togetherness are very far from providing conclusive reasons for the transfer of

3. The crucial work here is *Nationalism* by Elie Kedourie (London: Hutchinson, 1960).
4. *Nations and Nationalism Since 1780: Programme, Myth, Reality* (Cambridge: Cambridge University Press, 1990).
5. Ghita Ionescu, *Leadership in an Interdependent World: The Statesmanship of Adenauer, de Gaulle, Thatcher, Reagan and Gorbachev* (Harlow: Longman, 1991), viii.

power from nation-states to international organizations which the Olympian thinks advisable.

Any developing cluster of popular errors is likely to reveal to us that some new movement is afoot. In this case, the errors gain part of their plausibility from a set of terminological confusions, and our next business must be to clarify these.

Nationality Is Not the Same as Nation

Most of these confusions are related to the expression "nation-state." This expression is in one sense, of course, an absurdity. No state precisely corresponds to a nation, whatever a nation might be taken to be, and the classic nation-states whose political success as the central actors in European history gave rise to the vogue for nationalism are particularly implausible in this role. Britain, for example, contains at least four nations — the English, Welsh, Irish, and Scottish — and one must cautiously say "at least" because further shadowy nations hover on the periphery. The Cornish have sometimes claimed this status, and in the 1960s an office was set up in Manchester to promote the claims of Northumbria, one of the more resilient of the seven kingdoms of the Anglo-Saxon heptarchy. Similarly, France includes Bretons, Basques, and Alsatians, not to mention a significant cultural divide between the north and the south.

And yet: to the question What is your nationality? the correct answer is to be found in what is written in one's passport. "British" and "French" may not be descriptions of nations, but they certainly refer to nationalities whose linguistic and cultural unity constitutes a form of nationhood no less concrete than that of the nations of which they are composed. Here, as throughout this field, a terminological clarification corresponds to an important point of substance: namely, that it is states which create nationalities, and not nations which create states. Nationalist theory accords with the famous remark by Péguy: *Tout commence en mystique et finit en politique.* In the beginning is the nation, an unselfconscious cultural and linguistic nature waiting like Sleeping Beauty to be aroused by the kiss of politics. The common reality by contrast is that states create a basic unification which leads in time to the shared culture of a nationality.

States are independent actors on the international scene by virtue of national sovereignty, which is nationality equipped by the political process with the capacity of agency. It is this form of agency which has come under attack by the reinvigorated universalism of the late twentieth century.

What Is Olympianism?

Olympianism is a movement of thought and sentiment aiming to transfer power away from nationally sovereign states towards international organizations. It is a universalist doctrine holding that the decisions of nation-states are selfish expressions of collective egoism and must be replaced by decisions consonant with the interests of humanity. Such a statement of desirability is reinforced, however, by an assertion of inevitability: the world is now (so the Olympian doctrine runs) increasingly interdependent, and this fact entails the conclusion that the appropriate level of decision on all basic questions is global. The claim to *both* desirability and inevitability reveals that Olympianism is not merely a political proposal but (in embryo at least) a fully fledged ideological doctrine. The comprehensive solution to the problems of the world previously found in the untrammeled power of a revolutionary proletariat, or a liberated womanhood, or rule by experts and other such ideas is now to be made on behalf of the deliberations of international committees.

The plausibility of this doctrine rests upon the obvious fact that many conflicts, especially between different ethnic groups, seem insoluble in their own terms. Who should adjudicate when one state confronts another over which should control Ulster, Cyprus, Kashmir, etc.? The only alternative would seem to be the rule of might. But even adjudication does not fully solve the problem for it is likely to leave one party deeply dissatisfied. The ultimate solution would seem to be a withdrawal of passion from these parochialities in a recognition that humanity is the basic unit of political arrangement.

The shadowy agent on whom hopes rest for the solution of these problems is called "the international community," an expression which, combining two warm and positive terms, may well conjure into being over a generation or two the government necessary if a real international community is to develop. Stranger things have happened. The history of the European Community has demonstrated how effectively a visionary project can acquire teeth. In earlier generations, visionary projects of world government attracted intellectuals, but were often treated with mistrust by statesmen on the ground that if so comprehensive and unchallengeable a power turned out to be bad, it would be a disaster like no other. Better the curate's egg of dispersed power than the possibility of a global despotism. Organizations such as the League of Nations and the United Nations were therefore circumscribed in the powers given to them. The sociology of Western states today, however, is significantly different from the sociology of that earlier sceptical period. Far more people have become detached from the immediate realities of wealth and power. Those who work in education, administration, and the diffusion of information decide public matters very largely in terms of the abstract ideas that appeal to them. Such is the soil of Olympianism.

It is a mark of most universalisms in politics to be optimistic about the rationality of power. Just as many philosophers of the Enlightenment believed that the quickest route to a more rational world lay in persuading the absolute monarchs, who already had the power, that rational management of their realms was desirable, so Olympianism is marked by an entrenched optimism about both the wisdom and effectiveness of international organizations. It has been suggested, for example, that the communal conflict in Ulster is intractable because the British government is not thought by the parties to be impartial as an international organization would be. The most obvious feature of the conflict in Ulster, however, is that it is clearly insoluble in its own terms. The Olympian position assumes that there *must* be a rational solution to this as to every other political problem. An international agency speaking for reason would restructure the political relations of the British Isles. Universalists in the past, however, have never been so unworldly as to ignore the necessity for using power to guarantee what reason prescribes. Experience suggests that universalist belief can turn peculiarly brutal and ruthless with those who reject its conclusions. Both Jacobin and Bolshevik began by talking peace and ended by discarding thousands of human beings as unsuitable materials for the new order.

The "international community" is to our time what the cosmopolis of the ancients was to the disoriented citizenry of Greek cities who found themselves under the rule of oriental monarchies. It is a similarly Platonic republic laid up in heaven. And it is significant that the earliest uses of the expression occurred in appeals for help from Third World countries facing disaster, or from states in which communist rule had collapsed leaving only ruin behind it. What the "international community" referred to when it occurred in these appeals was the United States, and perhaps Europe and Japan, as a source of helpful funding. A sentimental term thus facilitated the deeply unsentimental business of Asian and African governments extracting cash from the West. Such a generic expression in the mouths of rulers who had long abused Western imperialists helped conceal the brutal realities of who was giving help to whom. This particular employment of the term also points to the fact that the very word "community" trails in its wake proposals for redistributing the world's wealth, such as those advanced in the Brandt Report. Olympianism is thus a project for improving the world not merely by solving conflicts (construed as basically ethnic) but also by raising living standards as wealth is moved from the rich to the poor. For it is an elementary move among fiscal imperialists to translate ethnic conflict into conflict resulting from inequality.

Olympianism and the Educated Middle Class

Who are the Olympians? They clearly constitute an important strand of contemporary public opinion, and they reveal themselves most obviously in their support for specific internationalist projects. Environmentalists are almost invariably Olympian because they know that international organizations are far more receptive to projects for cleaning up the globe than national governments, whose scepticism is reinforced by the fact that they must bear the financial and political costs of the operation. Feminists similarly find that international declarations of the rights dear to their hearts run far ahead of the disposition of national governments to pay for them. Olympians, like the early philosophes, understand themselves to be, paradoxically, the party of humanity. But if humanity is all of us, what are these people doing, who are but a part, and yet claim to speak for all of us? The answer is, of course, that they claim to have recognized rationally what the rest of us will ultimately come to accept. They represent the superior constituency of rationality which in the long run we must all come to inhabit. Olympians thus wear a variety of hats — as partisans of humanity, the planet, the oppressed, and so on.

The current condition of the world, including the distribution of its good things, has been basically determined by the energy and intelligence of previous generations, and there are plenty of people who do not find it good. Such critics include many intellectuals in Africa, Asia, and Latin America, and the spokesmen for the people called "minorities" in the West. Most such people want to *manage* the current world so as to remove its injustices and imperfections. Projects of this kind encounter, at the level of national political processes, a firm counter-pressure of vested interests. At the level of international organizations, by contrast, before committees dealing with abstract desirabilities, such projects are able to shine unshadowed by the harsh realities of cost. Here is a stage on which only ideal actors perform.

It is not the only stage in which the abstract ideal is dominant. Universities and governmental bureaucracies are also arenas in which the ideal has been largely detached from the realities which loom large in the wider world of wealth production. The Olympians, then, like their philosophe predecessors, tend to come from the educated middle classes. They are Mannheim's free-floating intellectuals whose abstract conclusions about the world are unbiased by the intrusion of particular interest.

Olympianism is thus a dream of managed global perfection most irresistibly attractive to those educated middle classes who are not directly involved in the production of wealth. In the late twentieth century, it has found two grand areas of national transcendence, and trouble lurks in the bifurcation. The first outlet is support for (and involvement in) the United Nations and other institutions of global regulation. The second is, in Europe, support for the European Community. This second project is immediately attractive to Olympians because it transcends the national state, and can be seen as a step on the way to full internationalism. Olympians who support the European Community may, however, be making a significant mistake, for supranationalism is very far from being the same as internationalism. It is pretty clear that the European Community conceals the ambition to play the role of a great power on the world stage, and its policy on such matters as global free trade is notably less internationalist than that of some of its individual members, such as Britain and the Scandinavian countries.

The Managerial Dynamic

What is the essence of Olympianism? The clue is given by the fact that the European Community prefers aid to trade. The Community, for example, gives aid both to Eastern Europe and (particularly) to the independent Third World countries which used to be part of its own European empires. But it also very elaborately bars from its own markets such things as agricultural products which would compete with European producers. The absurdity of a Europe whose sugar is from homegrown beets rather than from cheaper cane producers in the Third World — an entrenched accident dating from the days of Napoleon — illustrates the compatibility between managerial rationality and sheer irrationality in the policies pursued.

Olympianism, as a project for managing the world, is systematically hostile to initiative. Whate'er can be administered, if we may parody Alexander Pope, is best. Novelty, passion, genuine variety are all dangerous to the project of management. International trade is an example of what national governments find hard to control. Transnational corporations and managers of money have the power to escape from high tax regimes and the industrial regulation they find inconvenient by moving their operations to more hospitable regions. From the days of mercantilism, through socialism and communism, to the corporatism of the present, governments — with the enthusiastic support of less efficient producers — have been typically animated by the desire to achieve complete control over national resources. The more trade goes international, the more energetically will the managerial imperative seek to follow in order to subject everything to the project of an administered perfection.

We might well parody the Olympian position, especially where it takes an environmental form, by comparing it to the parental attitude which shouts at the children in the next room: "Whatever you're doing, stop it." In developing this characterization of the Olympian movement, we must no doubt enter a set of caveats recognizing that international cooperation is in many areas desirable, that there are genuine problems of the environment to be considered, and that organizations which coordinate our response to international crime and other evils are certainly desirable. These issues are appropriately decided by liberal democratic governments on their merits. But there is no ideal of action nor criterion of conduct which cannot be misused, and Olympianism is the exploitation of the pragmatic in the interests of the utopian.

One notable *topos* of the Olympian is that the increasing complexity of the world demands increased regulation, and the most persuasive aspect of the *topos* is a concern for safety. Here again we must agree that it is up to a point useful to have regulations seeking to guarantee the safety of drugs, toys, machines, etc. A world requiring constant alertness to danger would be pretty intolerable. It would be no less intolerable, however, to have a regulation covering every possibility of danger, no matter how remote. Safety and security are the watchwords of not only the cautious but also of those who seek power over us. A rising tide of control in the interests of safety (and longevity) is an unmistakable feature of contemporary life. Smoking and the drinking of alcohol are under attack, and those who rule us at a variety of levels are keen to give us wise advice on what we ought and ought not to eat and drink. Whereas it was once religious doctrine which used to attack our vices, it is now scientific findings which provide the platform from which governments control conduct. What does not change is the passion of administrators to extend the control they exercise over us.

Safety has been a notable ground used by the commissioners of the European Community to extend their regulatory scope. Tightening the screw of such regulations has been putting firms out of business in the more law-abiding European countries. But the principle of safety operates in a wider arena. The Olympic Games were established at the end of the last century less because more thought was desirable than because less war was. Sport as a moral substitute for war—an Olympic as well as an Olympian policy—was an early instance of the project of rendering human impulses relatively harmless.

National allegiances were another target of the Olympian movement. The aim was to find a harmless form of expression, and the solution was a recasting of the teaching of history in schools, and an emphasis on folklore and national dress. The Soviet Union was a pioneer in developing techniques of safe nationalism; culture was encouraged and politics strictly suppressed.[6] However futile this policy may now seem given the nationalist

6. For a discussion of this kind of universalism, see Kenneth Minogue and Beryl Williams, "Ethnic Conflict in the Soviet Union: The Revenge of Particularism," in *Thinking Theoretically About Soviet Nationalities: History and Comparison in the Study of the USSR,* ed. Alexander J. Motyl (New York: Columbia University Press, 1992), 225–42.

resurgence in what used to be the Soviet Union, safe politics may be seen as a precursor of the age of safe sex, and new attempts will be made to achieve it.

The general principle involved here is that anything which might have serious consequences for individuals must be taken over into governmental control. In these terms, welfare supplied by government prevents individuals from suffering the consequences of their own fecklessness. Substitute expressions of nationalist enthusiasm may similarly distract peoples from real conflict. The ultimate aim of a managed world is the elimination of serious consequences, and this cannot be attained merely by management at the national level. International organization is thus the last frontier of universalism. Its ultimate success would be a world in which the basic human activity would be the hobby.

A New Class?

In the analysis of emerging political movements, it is a familiar step to diagnose the growth of a new ascendent class, and my argument suggests that the prime bearer of Olympian sentiments would be the theorist-bureaucrat working for some international organization. If where one stands depends on where one sits, then the increasing numbers of people who work for international organizations, and the much wider group who consider their destinies entwined with such institutions, will be steadily detaching themselves from their national loyalty. Much wider still is the class of those educated in modern Western universities whose only current conception of academic objectivity is a mechanical distancing of oneself from one's inherited culture. Academic education in many Western universities has been politicized so as to constitute a kind of civics course which "de-nationalizes" students and prepares them for citizenship of a state which does not yet exist — the international community of the future. A shallow philosophical moralizing now directs idealism towards international organizations, most of which have not yet been put to the test. This is a safer lodgment for a political aspiration than any actual society, for as Burke sardonically remarked: "No difficulties occur in what has never been tried."

The new class of theorist-administrator is distinguished by possession of an international culture. Dress, language, tastes, and much else serve to homogenize the Olympian, from whom a comprehensive ecumenism has rubbed any rough edges of cultural particularity. This feature of modern life is perhaps less obvious in the West than elsewhere, because it is of course Western customs and attitudes which constitute the decor of this new internationalist culture. It is much more obvious among African and Asian cosmopolitans because it sometimes puts them dramatically at odds with the people they rule. It is important to realize that the ubiquity of an internationalist culture does not really diminish the starkness of conflict between different interests at the global level. All it actually does is dress each interest up in universal finery, and ultimately it will make conflicts of interest more intractable than before. For interests may compromise, but universal principles must fight it out without giving quarter.

For the moment, however, Olympianism moderates these clashes because the power of international organizations is largely limited to recommendation. Declaration of ideals is relatively costless at this level and statesmen may outdo each other in devotion to abstract human betterment. International organizations thus provide the oxygen of aspiration which keeps burning the fires of moral managerialism in the national states of the West.

Olympianism and the Future of Democracy

Let me summarize by saying that the "collective egoism" of ethnic conflict is *not* sole cause of the problems of international order. The resurgence of this false belief signals a new phase of the universalist ambition to manage human diversity in terms of some rational project. Two contradictory impulses are at war in the bosom of the West: first, an inclination to explore individuality both in private and in institutional forms; secondly, a yearning for a communal harmony which would require strong management at the center. It seems unlikely that either of these impulses will weaken in the near future, and their most violent clash in the recent past — in the form of the communist repression of all individual initiative — has left us with the belief that freedom is safe. In fact, however, the managerial impulse has simply taken a new form, and one that is peculiarly insidious because every stage of its progress can ride piggyback on pragmatic desirabilities.

Olympianism is a form of moral enthusiasm which affirms that *all* conflicts are rationally solvable at the universal level of international organizations. Confusing nation with nationality, it has denigrated the worth of all local loyalties and induced in many a contempt for the culture to which they belong. It has also begun to create a new class, and an eclectic culture distinct from the original cultures of the world. One emerging consequence of this process is that internationalized statesmen come to constitute a self-referring club potentially at odds with their own electorates. It is a very superior club, whose members rather look down on those outside it — the very electorates whom they represent. Those electorates are not infrequently beginning to repay that contempt by holding politicians in low esteem. Olympianism is thus an important component in the crisis of democratic politics which many commentators have begun to notice.

The First Person Plural

ROGER SCRUTON

POLITICAL ORDER, I maintain, depends upon the existence of a community that identifies itself as "we." Since there is no "we" without a "they," the possibility of enmity and fragmentation is contained in the very foundation of political existence. However, this does not imply that all communities are equally threatening to their neighbors, or that there is no way of achieving by negotiation and compromise the stable frontiers and sense of belonging that former societies have reached, as a rule, through war.

A survey of recent literature on nations and nationalism — and in particular literature produced by those, whether leftish or liberal, who have cast aspersions on the national idea — suggests the following broad consensus:

(a) Nations are comparatively recent phenomena, emerging perhaps with the Enlightenment, or as a consequence of the Industrial Revolution, or (more plausibly) through the dissemination of the written word by what Benedict Anderson calls "print capitalism."[1]

(b) Nations are not the "natural" communities implied in the various doctrines and theories of nationalism, but as much the creatures as the creators of the states that are conjoined to them. Sometimes a "nation" is created by a colonial administration, with its arbitrary division of the spoils of imperial trade; sometimes it is created by a language, or a religion; but the common language and the common religion may themselves be the result of administrative convenience, just like the nation which is supposedly enshrined in them. In Gellner's words (quoted with approval by Eric Hobsbawm): "Nations as a natural, God-given way of classifying men, as an inherent though long-delayed political destiny, are a myth; nationalism, which sometimes takes preexisting cultures and turns them into nations, sometimes invents them, and often obliterates preexisting cultures: *that* is a reality."[2]

1. Benedict Anderson, *Imagined Communities,* 2nd ed. (London: Verso, 1991).
2. Ernest Gellner, *Nations and Nationalism* (Oxford: Basil Blackwell, 1983). Eric Hobsbawm, *Nations and Nationalism Since 1780* (Cambridge: Cambridge University Press, 1990).

(c) Nationalism is therefore the *ideology* of the modern state: the set of doctrines and beliefs which sanctify this peculiar local arrangement, and legitimize the new forms of government and administration that have emerged in the modern world. Ernest Gellner even goes so far as to describe nationalism as a philosophy of the book: the instrument by which the new bureaucrats sought to legitimize their rule in post-Enlightenment Europe, by affirming an identity between the people and the literate intellectuals who are alone competent to govern them. Nationalism, which attempts to form a sacred history from the fact of language itself, privileges writing over the spoken tongue, and official idiom over local dialect — since it is in the official idiom that the nation as a whole can live. There is no better ideology for persuading the common man that he owes his loyalty to educated and anonymous pen-pushers in the distant cities, rather than to the local aristocrat whose power has been forever dissipated by the industrial process.

(d) Nations are "imagined communities," in Benedict Anderson's memorable phrase.[3] That is, they are communities which arise partly from a representation of themselves, and which include members who never meet, and have nothing in common besides their membership, and the shared destiny implied in it.

I say that those views express a broad consensus among skeptics; but it is not only liberal and left-leaning writers who have defended them. The theory that the nation is a creation of the modern state, and not vice versa, was first articulated, to my knowledge, by Lord Acton[4]; the theory of the nation as a modern invention, and of nationalism as a functional ideology designed to legitimize postimperial power, has been advocated by Elie Kedourie and Kenneth Minogue,[5] both conservative thinkers. And I have defended a view of the nation as a community founded on its own self-conception — though without the benefit of Benedict Anderson's beautifully described examples.[6] So maybe a received idea of nationhood is beginning to emerge among people of all political persuasions. According to this idea, the nation is a peculiarly modern form of community, and one whose emergence is inseparable from the culture of the written word. Of course, the "modern" world is an amorphous idea, and many of the features that are ascribed to nationality can be found, embryonically at least, in the literature of Greece and Rome. (*The Battle of Maldon* also springs to mind: what is

---

3. Anderson, *Imagined Communities.*
4. John Emerich Edward Dalberg-Acton, 1st Baron, "Nationality," in *The History of Freedom and Other Essays,* ed. J. N. Figgis and R. V. Lawrence (London: Macmillan, 1907), 273–74.
5. Elie Kedourie, *Nationalism* (London: Hutchinson, 1960). Kenneth Minogue, *Nationalism* (London: B. T. Batsford, 1967).
6. Roger Scruton, "In Defence of the Nation," in *The Philosopher on Dover Beach* (Manchester, England: Carcanet, 1990), 299–329.

that, if not *national* literature?) But it is surely indisputable that when we *now* discuss the nation, and the ideas through which it is described, condemned, and defended, we refer to an arrangement that is inconceivable without the process of modern history.

Much of the recent literature has involved implied criticisms, not only of nationalism as an ideology, but also of the national idea through which the imagined community is formed, of the nation that results from it, and of the nation-state as a form of political order. We ought therefore to ask what the nation *does* for its members: what emotional, moral, social, and political benefits it supposedly confers on them, whether they need those benefits, and whether they might be supplied from another source. And if—as its critics suggest—the nation is the source of so much violence, hatred, and suspicion, we ought to enquire whether it might nevertheless exist without that violence, hatred, and suspicion, or whether they might be gradually moderated and subjected to some legal or administrative cure.

None of those issues can be explored, I believe, if we do not understand the topic to which I address myself: the "we" of membership. I have called this the first person plural, in order to emphasize its close connection to those forms of association — language, kinship, religion, and the occupation of land—through which people become conscious of the distinction between "us" and "them." When it is argued that nations are artificial communities, it should be remembered that there are two kinds of social artifact: those which are the objects of a decision—as when people join together in a partnership—and those which arise "by an invisible hand," and as the result of decisions which in no way intend them. And I suspect that, when people balk at the suggestion that the nation is *as such* an artificial community, it is because they recognize that at least some nations arise spontaneously, as England did, and that only *some* nations are the direct result of an intention to produce them. Perhaps postcolonial and postimperial nations are produced by fiat—although that would be hotly disputed, I imagine, by just about every inhabitant of the former Soviet Empire. And even when there *is* a conscious decision, the nation that emerges will seldom be the entity intended, but will be shaped by the very same invisible hand that has obeyed the "cunning of reason" from time immemorial. This is obviously true of the world's greatest artificial nation: the United States of America, which is by no means the entity intended by the Founding Fathers. Interestingly, it is America, among the nations of the modern world, that has the most vivid personality, and the greatest ability to inspire love and hatred among those who encounter it. But is it the American *state* or the American *nation* that is the true object of this love and hatred, and the true bearer of personality?

The example illustrates what is principally in the mind of those who believe that nations are artifacts: namely that they result from political organization; and this political organization is distinctly modern in character, involving impersonal and secular forms of administration, which do not require of their subjects anything more than their registration in the book of citizens. *What* results from the relevant political decisions may of course be quite other than the decisions intend; and the rich admixture of history and community that occurs when people are stirred together in the crucible of a modern state is surely nothing that even *could* have been intended by those whose actions were the first cause of its existence.

So understood, a nation could be contrasted with two other forms of continuity: the tribe or kinship group, and what Spengler calls the "creed-community."[7] The first is often described as "natural," meaning that it arises spontaneously, and is never the result of a decision — certainly not of a political decision. Members of a tribe are joined by marriage and kinship, and the first person plural is coextensive with the sense of kin. It might be suggested that tribes are distinguished from nations not only by the closeness of the ties between their members, but also by the fact that the members are personally known to one another. But this would be too simple, for two reasons. First, tribes can grow and take on a quasi-political structure, as their members move to foreign parts or lose touch with the ancestral community. (Consider the exemplary history of the Jews.) Secondly, the majority of members of the tribe are either dead or unborn, and yet *just as much members* as those who happen to be temporarily living. This is precisely what relations of kinship mean: that you and I are descended from a common source, and owe our membership to the fact that our common ancestor is also still a member. All tribal ceremonies in which membership is at stake — marriages, funerals, births, initiations — are also attended by the dead, who in turn are the guardians of those unborn. And the consolation of membership resides precisely in this union with absent generations, through which the fear of death is allayed and the individual granted the supreme endorsement of existing as a limb of the eternal organism.

The creed-community grows naturally from the tribe, just as religion grows naturally from tribal conceptions of membership. Through ceremonies of membership, in which the dead bear witness to our need of them, the gods enter the world. Every invocation of the dead is a transition to the supernatural; and whatever it is that people worship is located in the supernatural sphere: which is not to say that it is "outside" nature, or in any way inaccessible. On the contrary, the gods of the tribesman are as real and near to him as the spirits of his ancestors, and may be carried around in tangible

7. Oswald Spengler, *The Decline of the West* (2 vols.), vol. 2, on the "Magian" culture; trans. Charles Francis Atkinson (New York: Alfred A. Knopf, 1926–1928), 233–61.

form. But that too is a sign of their supernatural character; for only what is supernatural can be *identical* with its own representation, as the god is identical with the idol, which exists in a hundred replicas. (This should be borne in mind by those who notice the close relation between the nation and the symbols [flag, anthem, sacred texts] that represent it.)

The creed-community is, however, distinct from the tribe. For here the criterion of membership has ceased to be kinship, and become worship and obedience. Now there is a new, and in a sense artificial, test of membership. Those who worship my gods, and accept the same divine prescriptions, are joined to me by this, even though we are strangers. Moreover, creed-communities extend their claims beyond the living, just as tribal societies do. The dead have acquired the privileges of the worshiper through our prayers. But the dead are present in these new ceremonies on very different terms: they no longer have the authority of the tribal ancestors; rather they are subjects of the same divine overlord, undergoing their reward or punishment in conditions of greater proximity to the ruling power. They throng together in the great unknown, just as we will, released from every earthly tie and united by faith.

Creed-communities can expand beyond the kinship relation most easily when they enjoy a sacred text, in which the truths about the deity and his demands on us are set down for all time. The existence of such a text sanctifies the language in which it is written: the language is lifted out of time and change, and becomes immemorial, like the voice of God. (The etymology of "sanskrit" should not be forgotten.) Hence true creed-communities resist not only changes to the ceremonies (which define the experience of membership), but also changes to the sacred text and to the language used in recording it. By this means Hebrew, Arabic, Latin, and the English of King James I have been lifted out of history and immortalized. Membership of the creed-community may often require an apprenticeship in the sacred language: certainly no priest can be allowed to ignore it. But the creed-community inevitably grants privileges to the *native* speakers of that language, and endows them with a weapon that permits them to rule the world (or at least the only bit of the world that matters — the world of the faithful).

The initial harmony between tribal and credal criteria of membership gives way to conflict, as the rival forces of family love and religious friendship exert themselves over small communities. This conflict is the motor of Islamic history, and can be witnessed all over the Middle East, where local creed-communities have grown out of the monotheistic religions in accordance with a tribal experience of membership. There is at least one such community — the Druze — in which a credal idea of membership has come to depend on a tribal criterion. Each child of a Druze is held to be a member of the sect solely by virtue of his birth, and each new member of the sect is believed to inherit the soul of a Druze that died. The community can neither grow nor dwindle, but is an eternal communion of the unborn and the dead, each member of which is simultaneously in both conditions, while also being alive!

Rather than divert ourselves with the infinite variations on the two paradigms of tribal and credal membership, let us turn to the modern world, in which these pre-political forms of social order enter into relation with the requirements of government. For a long time Europe existed as a kind of creed-community — but one in which sovereignty had crystallized in the hands of individual families, whose claims were either endorsed by the pope or asserted against him. But Christianity was a creed-community with a difference. From its beginning in the Roman Empire it internalized some of the ideas of imperial government; in particular, it adopted and immortalized the greatest of all Roman achievements, which was the universal system of law as a means for the resolution of conflicts and for the administration of distant provinces. Although Islam also has its law, it is explicitly a holy law, laying down the path to salvation. Moreover, it derives its authority exclusively from the past, either from the word of God as recorded in the Koran or from the exemplary acts of the prophet, as related in the Sunna. Jurisprudence is limited to the art of tracing a decision back to those authoritative sources, or to some hadith of the prophet which will fill the lacuna. The Roman law by contrast was secular, and unconcerned with the individual's religious well-being. It was an instrument for governing people regardless of their credal differences; and its decisions were not validated by tracing them to some sacred source, but by autonomous principles of judicial reasoning based on an explicit statement of the law. The law itself could change in obedience to changing circumstances; and its validity derived purely from the fact that it was commanded by the sovereign power, and enforced against every subject.

That conception of law, which we tend to associate with the Enlightenment only because it was then reasserted without the encrustation of religious doctrine that had in the interim grown around it, is perhaps the most important force in the emergence of the European forms of sovereignty. It ensured the development of law as an entity independent of the sovereign's command, and the maintenance of a universal jurisdiction through the courts of canon law. At the same time, each sovereign, through his own courts, was able to qualify and narrow the universal law, so that it slowly adapted itself to his territorial claims. Thus there arose the idea of kingdoms, not as local power centers but as territorial jurisdictions, whose monarchs were constrained by the law and appointed by it, as well as empowered to change it in their favor. Often the law was, as in England, the creation of judges: and the common law principles (including those of equity) have ensured that, wherever the English law has prevailed, it is law and not the executive power that has the last word in any conflict between them.

These facts were incorporated into the European idea of a sovereign state, in which territorial jurisdiction has had at least as much importance as language and religion in shaping people's attachments. With the breakdown of the credal community in Europe, three distinct conceptions of membership exerted their forces over the popular imagination, in order to generate the new first person plural. First religion, and in particular those fine differences of doctrine and practice which distinguished Catholic from Protestant, and sect from sect. (Note that fine differences are always more important in determining membership than large differences, precisely because they permit comparisons. The man whose religion differs from mine by a tiny article, or a barely perceivable gesture, is not a believer in other gods, but a blasphemer against my gods. Unlike the man with other deities, he is automatically an object of hostility; he is the enemy within.) Secondly language, and in particular the languages which had attained sanctity, through some authoritative translation of the sacred texts (for instance English and German), and which had been dispersed among strangers by the art of printing. Thirdly, the gravitational force of territorial jurisdictions, under which contracts could be enforced, disputes settled, marriages and institutions legalized, with uniform effect over a continuous territory.

This third form of membership is often forgotten. But it should be borne in mind by anyone who wishes to understand the foundation of the modern British nation, from the successive incorporation of jurisdictions (and also rival legal systems) under a single crown. The union with Scotland took effect by a legal process whose effects could not be avoided, once James IV of Scotland had ascended the English throne. Even if other differences — kinship and religion — remained; and even if the idiolect of Scotland was a spur to separatist intentions: the British nation (which at first called itself an "empire") was an inevitable result of the juridical process. It would be wrong to call this process political, since the new state resulted from it and did not produce it. Moreover, the autonomy of our jurisdictions gives them their own motivating power.

But there is a very different conception of membership associated with the territorial jurisdiction. The law treats the individual as a bearer of rights and duties; it recasts his relations with his neighbor in abstract terms; it shows a preference for contract over status, and for definable interests over inarticulate bonds. In short, it is a great *reformer* of membership, tending always in a contractual direction. It loosens our ties, precisely by making them judiciable and therefore articulate. This is why the law has so little effect in private life outside Europe — and less effect in Europe the further south one goes. Disputes among Arab tribes are frequently settled privately, by individual acts of revenge; contracts are not really contracts, but solemn vows of friendship, whose breach is punished by war. Rarely is a judge's decision accepted as final, unless the parties are largely indifferent to the outcome.

Nevertheless, we must not think of jurisdiction as merely a conventional arrangement: a kind of ongoing and severable agreement, of the kind that appealed to the Social Contract thinkers of the Enlightenment. It involves a genuine "we" of membership: not as visceral as that of kinship; not as uplifting as that of worship; and not as inescapable as that of language and kinship; but a "we" all the same. For a jurisdiction gains its validity either from an immemorial past, or from a fictitious contract between people who already *belong together.* In the English case, our law comes with the authority of long usage; our ancestors speak as clearly through it as they speak through the King James Bible; and it owes its authority to the fact that those subject to it are, by that very fact, incorporated into a community beyond the living, in which the dead and the unborn are also represented.

In the American case, in which a decision was made to adopt a constitution and make a jurisdiction *ab initio,* it is nevertheless true that a first person plural was involved in the very making. This is confessed to in the document itself: "We, the people . . ." Which people? Why, *us;* we who *already belong,* whose historic tie is now to be transcribed into law. Indeed, if we think about the various liberal theories of the state, which have tried to imagine a society composed entirely of freely consenting individuals, bound solely by the contract between them, we find that we can make sense of the idea only on the assumption of some such precontractual "we." For who is to be included in the contract? And why? And what do we do with the one who opts out? The obvious answer is that the founders of the new social order already belong together: they have already "imagined" themselves as a community. They have already begun that long process of self-representation which enables them to determine who should participate in the future, and who should not. Furthermore, the social contract makes sense only if future generations are already included in it. Our purpose is to establish a society: and at once there arises that web of noncontractual obligations — the web of piety — which links parents to children and children to parents, and which ensures willy-nilly that within a generation our society will be encumbered by nonvoting members, dead and unborn, who will rely on something other than a mere contract between the living if their rights are to be respected and their love deserved. Even when there arises, as in America, an idea of "elective nationality," so that newcomers may choose to belong, *what* is chosen is precisely not a contract but a bond of membership, whose obligations and privileges transcend anything that could be contained in a defeasible agreement. (Compare Hegel's view of marriage: it begins in contract, but a contract to surpass the realm of contract.)

Now there cannot be a society, I contend, without this nonpolitical experience of membership. For it is this which enables me to regard the interests and needs of strangers as *my* concern; which enables me to recognize the authority of decisions and laws that I must obey, even though they are not directly in my interest; which gives me a criterion to distinguish those who are entitled to the benefit of the sacrifices that my membership calls from me, from those who are interloping. Take away the experience of membership and it is every man for himself; moreover, the dead will be disenfranchised, and the unborn, of whom the dead are the metaphysical guardians, will be deprived of their inheritance. The mere "contract between the living" is a contract to squander the earth's resources for the benefit of its temporary residents. A society founded on such a principle will last for a generation at most, and its destruction will be a moral good.

Such a first person plural is of course what the various national ideas have tried to recapture, in circumstances where bonds of kinship have faded and the creed-community has been usurped by sovereign powers, whether indigenous or imperial. And before evaluating the project, it is important to distinguish two kinds of nation: those that have grown under the aegis of European jurisdictions, and those that have been thrown up by the collapse of empires. England, which gradually became Britain, is an example of the first; Nigeria an example of the second. Between these two are many intermediate cases: the Czech nation, for instance. Moreover, among those whose identity has been formed by the breakup of empires, we should distinguish a variety of cases: those which had no pre-imperial identity, other than the identities of the tribes or creed-communities that inhabited the region; those which had a pre-imperial history as nations, and perhaps even as nation-states (such as Poland); and those which gradually acquired some elements of nationhood, as a result of a decentralizing process based on linguistic, religious, or ethnic premises. Finally we should distinguish among empires, between those based purely on coercion, like the Mogul and Soviet Empires, and those in which the rule of law is the norm, such as the Hapsburg and British Empires in their final years. All those distinctions are important, since they remind us that the phenomenon that we know as the nation may not be a single phenomenon; and that the various attempts by the peoples of the modern world to realize their instinctive sense of membership in a political structure may not be attempts in a single direction.

When considering a nation like my own, I am struck immediately by a remarkable fact. Although England grew as part of the creed-community of Christendom, it has never (pilgrimages notwithstanding) experienced itself as united with that community in a true first person plural. Always the rest of Christendom has been to some extent "other." This has something to do with the nature of the British Isles (even though England is only a part of them), something to do with the habit of seafaring, something to do with the weather (as Montesquieu argued), and a lot to do with the nature of English common law. Long before the Reformation our Church defined itself as *English;* it was never wholly under the yoke of Rome; nor did the transition to Anglicanism seem unnatural to a great many of the people — horrible though it was for those priests and religious who remained loyal to their vows. In effect the religious obedience of the English people became a by-product of the national community. And this process occurred very early: it was in motion before the development of printing; it accelerated at the Reformation, and created in the pastoral England of the early eighteenth century a remarkable society in which religious affiliation followed national (and sometimes local) loyalties, rather than vice versa.

The most important forces in this process were law and territory. Island territories have boundaries defined by nature; they force upon us, through the dangerous adventure on the seas, the vivid distinction between home and abroad. Our weather and climate, and the patterns of agriculture that are required by them, produced a unique landscape which reinforced this feeling. And the experience of a settled jurisdiction, defined by territory, encouraged Englishmen to define their rights and liberties from the very beginning. The result was an experience of safety, quite different from that of the tribe, but connected with the sense that we belong in this *place,* and that our ancestors and children belong here too. Evidently the common language reinforced the feeling: but to suppose that we could have enjoyed these territorial, legal, and linguistic hereditaments, and yet refrained from becoming a nation, representing itself to itself as entitled to these things, and defining even its religion in terms of them, is to give way to fantasy. In no way can the emergence of the English nation, as a form of membership, be regarded as a product of Enlightenment universalism, or the Industrial Revolution, or the administrative needs of a modern bureaucracy. It existed before those things, and also shaped them into powerful instruments of its own.

The case may be different with the nations that are formed in *defiance* of imperial powers. But we should remember that, however flimsy the narratives which form their titles to legitimacy, they invariably summon up old and ancestral things. Even when the reference to these things is a myth, or an "invented tradition" of the kind that historians have made familiar, it serves the purpose of affirming membership. The nation is not, even in these cases, conceived as an accidental and defeasible contract between strangers; it is a hereditary entitlement, a burden of duty, and a call to sacrifice. Unlike a contract, the bond of membership is disinterested: I am *given* to it, and it to me, by the very fact of my existence. My debt to the nation is a debt of gratitude and piety—and the fact that this point has never been better expressed than by a Roman poet should remind us that, however transient this or that form of nationhood might be, the need to which it ministers is a human universal. Benedict Anderson puts the point well: "If historians, diplomats, politicians, and social scientists are quite at ease with the idea of 'national interest,' for most ordinary people of whatever class the whole point of the nation is that it is interestless. Just for that reason, it can ask for sacrifices."[8]

When we consider the nations of Central Europe, we should bear two things in mind: first, that there really are nonpolitical relations which cause them to divide—distinctions of language, of religion, of custom, and of race (where "race" denotes a *perception*—an "intentional" rather than a "natural" kind); secondly, that they have not enjoyed, for the last fifty years, what they once enjoyed under the Hapsburg Empire, namely a territorial jurisdiction based on law, which enabled conflicts to be settled without violence. The reestablishment of a territorial jurisdiction, without which there cannot be a state in the modern sense, requires, if I am right, the simultaneous or prior affirmation of a first person plural. Without the bond of membership, obligations to strangers will not be honored, and the law will be regarded as alien. But a territorial jurisdiction requires territory, and the title to that territory cannot be based on the law which has yet to be invented. It must therefore be based on whatever narratives of membership can carry conviction: and that *is* the process whereby nations, in these circumstances, are formed.

I do not regard the U.S.A. as an exception to the view that nonpolitical experiences of membership are necessary for the flourishing of a modern state. What is remarkable about the United States, however, is its ability to welcome new members, an ability which itself derives from the narrative whereby "we the people" once laid claim to the land. This land is ours because we came here in flight from our tormenters. Let us not despise those who come here in their turn.

Even though Abraham Lincoln declared the American "nation" to be distinct from others, in being founded on a "covenant," he did not mean to discard the national idea, but on the contrary to endorse it. Modern presidents and politicians make free use of this idea, and almost all children are

8. Anderson, *Imagined Communities,* 144.

inducted into citizenship by means of it. The most rebellious of leftist journals in the U.S. calls itself *The Nation,* in order to emphasize that the country has a *national* and not just a political interest, and that the left is its true custodian.

America is first of all a territory, possessed through a "union" of states. It has a common language, common habits of association, common customs, and a common Judaeo-Christian culture. It is intensely patriotic, and — in its healthy part — determined to defend its interests against the world. As Tocqueville observed, the process of association is hyperactive in the United States, proliferating its "little platoons" which add their fund of local loyalties to the larger loyalty upon which the political order depends. (Think of the American football matches, with their quasi-Pindaric sense that the community and its gods are here immortalized.) There is also a strong religious dimension to the American idea. A strange hybrid monotheism has grown from the thousand churches of America — Christian in form, Hebrew in content — and each new generation is absorbed into it by the process of national loyalty. And this loyalty has its own historical myths, its own "dreams," its own sense of mission, its own powerful self-image, in which the American land is the last refuge of the dispossessed, and also the birthplace of a new and unfettered enterprise.[9]

I do not say that the national loyalty is shared by *all* Americans. But whoever travels away from the universities (centers of disaffection in any state) will discover a process of nation-building that is second to none in the modern world. And those who stand outside the national loyalty — who attack their country's traditions and ridicule its culture; who scoff at its simplicity, despise its leaders, and reject its God; who, in short, repudiate the bond of membership — who are they, in general, if not the new clerks, who seek to write the history of nations yet again, so as to justify their own ascendancy within it?

And this brings me to an interesting point. Although, if I am right, the experience of membership has survived into the modern world, and the nation, in its various forms, is the best that we have as an expression of it, we should distinguish two forms of the first person plural: the "we" of affirmation, and the "we" of denial. No society can survive, I contend, or ought to survive, if it cannot generate the "we" of affirmation: the assertion of itself as entitled to its land and institutions, inheriting them from its ancestors and passing them on. This affirmative "we" does not express a contract among living members, but precisely the refusal to be limited by contract. It involves an invocation of ancestors and progeny, as implicated in our present acts. It is the principal way in which the community represents (or "imagines") itself as enduring through time: by deriving its rights

9. The previous two paragraphs are adapted from Scruton, "In Defence of the Nation," in *The Philosopher on Dover Beach,* 323–24.

and duties from circumstances that were never chosen, and from bonds that are irrevocable since absent generations, who cannot consent to their renegotiation, are nevertheless as much bound by them as we.

But there is a "we" of denial, which grows as the bond of membership weakens. Perhaps we do not have a right to this territory; perhaps our ancestors gained possession of it by unjust and cruel acts; perhaps there is nothing of value in the institutions that they have passed to us; perhaps law, religion, and morality as we know them are merely the masks of usurping power. Thus there grows a new kind of narrative of the nation: a "narrative in deconstruction," in which the whole story is told again as a story of crime. This is indeed what you see in such historians as Robert Hughes, whose *The Fatal Shore* was calculated to rob the Australians of the last vestige of pride in their inheritance; or in countless works of school history in Britain, which write only of the Empire, and the regime of racism and slavery on which it was supposedly founded. Frequently these counter-narratives are offered (for example by Emmanuel Wallerstein and André Gunder Frank) as reprimands: and often the conclusion is drawn that we should now allocate part of our resources, or maybe the whole of them, to bettering the situation of those peoples in the Third World who, but for our exploitation, would today be heirs to that which we stole from them.

I do not wish to adjudicate between the affirmers and the deniers; but I should like to point out that the "we" of denial, so important in shaping the politics of our most modern nation-states, is also a "we" of membership — asserting relations of obligation and responsibility between the living and the dead; asking us to bear the burden of our ancestors' misdeeds, and to recognize moral bonds for which we never contracted, towards victims who were no victims of ours. The very same urge, to find our identity by immersing ourselves in a historic community stretching across all the generations, and bound by territory, language, and jurisdiction into a corporate whole, manifests itself just as much in those who scoff at the nation as it does in those who willingly accept its transcendental demands.

Nor is this surprising. For we are social beings, who can exist and behave as autonomous agents only because we are supported in our ventures by that feeling of primal safety which the bond of society brings. We can envisage no project and no satisfaction on which the eyes of others do not shine. We are joined to those others, and even when they are strangers to us, they are also part of us. It is the indispensable need for membership that brings the national idea to our minds; and there is no rational argument that will expel it, once it is there. Without it, we are homeless; and even if our attitude to home is one of sour disaffection, home is no less necessary to our sense of who we are.

But what must we do to avert the bellicose threats that grow alongside those idylls of love and gusts of *ressentiment*? If there is no "we" without a "they," how can we avoid the rivalry that will lead to war? I will conclude with a suggestion.

Those critics of the nation who have seen in it the root of xenophobia and racism, have often disparaged the imperial powers of Europe for their indecent contempt towards the "natives" of their territories. A picture has developed — by no means wholly wrong — of European despots, smugly convinced of their ancestral right of sovereignty, cruelly trampling on people whom they regarded as their genetic inferiors. But these very same critics are frequently enthusiastic supporters of the "national liberation struggles," whereby colonial peoples attempt to affirm themselves as nations, and to achieve independence in precisely that guise. Of course, the new nations are not the same kind of thing as the old ones, as I have argued. But they answer to the same need: the need for a bond of membership that will conform to the geographical and administrative realities, which will permit the dead and the unborn to stand beside us, and which will define our territory as home.

Now you can't have it both ways. If nationhood is a boon to the people of New Guinea and Peru, it must also be a boon to those who formerly oppressed them. The only question, therefore, is how nations can live side by side with enough local loyalty and territorial privilege to define themselves, and yet with the procedures and customs that encourage them to settle their disputes through negotiation and not through war. One solution is this: the growth of a single jurisdiction, incorporating the local jurisdictions, while conceding their administrative autonomy, and upholding a strict rule of law, enforced against all wrongdoers. Such a rule of law is unlikely, perhaps even inconceivable, without a metropolitan power, which will ensure that jurisdiction will not fragment along ethnic or religious boundaries. In other words, it will tend towards Empire, in one of its forms: the form which the Romans and the British imagined themselves to be administering, and which the Hapsburg Dual Monarchy administered in Central Europe. Those who, growing from such empires, express themselves now with the "we" of denial, denouncing the nation-states which emerged from the ruins, ought perhaps to think how we might restore those empires, so as to establish genuine rules of law, and a metropolitan sovereignty, over peoples who — thanks perhaps to the imperial legacy — have proved unable to govern themselves.

I am very grateful to Charles Griswold for comments on an earlier draft of this paper.

BERNARD LEVIN

Chief columnist of *The Times* (London) since 1971, and a full-time journalist since 1953, Bernard Levin was educated at Christ's Hospital and the London School of Economics and Political Science. His publications include the collections of journalism *If You Want My Opinion* (1992), *Now Read On* (1990), *All Things Considered* (1988), *In These Times* (1986), *The Way We Live Now* (1984), *Speaking Up* (1982), and *Taking Sides* (1979). Each of his three travel books has been adapted into a television series: *A Walk Up Fifth Avenue* (1989), *To the End of the Rhine* (1987), and *Hannibal's Footsteps* (1985). His first book was *The Pendulum Years* (1971), published in the United States as *Run It Down the Flagpole,* a social-cultural history of the 1960s. He is also author of *Enthusiasms* (1983). Mr. Levin has been a television, theatre, and literary critic, and has written and broadcast for radio and television. He was made a Companion of the British Empire in 1990.

SIMON SCHAMA

Professor of History and Mellon Professor of the Social Sciences at Harvard University, and Senior Research Associate at the Minta de Guenzburg Center for European Studies at Harvard University, Simon Schama studied history at Cambridge University, where from 1966 to 1976 he was a Fellow of Christ's College. He has also been a Fellow and Tutor in Modern History at Brasenose College, Oxford, and Erasmus Lecturer in the Civilization of the Netherlands at Harvard University. He is the author of *Patriots and Liberators: Revolution in the Netherlands 1780–1813* (1977), *Two Rothschilds and the Land of Israel* (1979), and *The Embarrassment of Riches: An Interpretation of Dutch Culture in the Golden Age* (1987). Most recently Professor Schama published a historical novel entitled *Dead Certainties (Unwarranted Speculations)* (1991).

DONALD S. CARNE-ROSS

University Professor, William Goodwin Aurelio Professor of Greek Language and Literature, and Professor of Classics and Modern Languages at Boston University, Donald S. Carne-Ross has an M.A. from Oxford University. He has written extensively on translation and about the "points of intersection" among different languages and cultures, and between the present and the past. He has also written extensively on classical Greek, English, and Italian literature. His books include *Instaurations: Essays In and Out of Literature* and *Pindar,* and he is currently working on a book about Sophocles. He is cofounder of *Arion: A Journal of Humanities and the Classics* and of *Delos,* the journal of the National Translation Center.

HUGH TREVOR-ROPER

Educated at Charterhouse and Christ Church, Oxford, Hugh Trevor-Roper was Research Fellow at Merton College, Regius Professor of Modern History and subsequently Fellow of Oriel College, Oxford, and Master of Peterhouse, Cambridge. He has been director of *The Times* Newspapers Ltd. His books include *Archbishop Laud* (1940); *The Last Days of Hitler* (1947); *The Gentry, 1540–1640* (1953); *Hitler's Table Talk* (editor, 1953); *Historical Essays* (1957); *The Rise of Christian Europe* (1965); *Religion, The Reformation and Social Change* (1967); *The Philby Affair* (1968); *The European Witch-Craze of the 16th and 17th Centuries* (1970); *The Plunder of the Arts in the Seventeenth Century* (1970); *Princes and Artists* (1976); *A Hidden Life* (1976); *Renaissance Essays* (1985); and *Catholics, Anglicans, and Puritans* (1987).

BEN WHITAKER

A barrister and Extra-Mural Lecturer in Law, London University, Ben Whitaker has been Director of the Gulbenkian Foundation since 1988. He has also been Executive Director of the Minority Rights Group, the U.K. member of the United Nations Human Rights Sub-Commission, Member of Parliament for Hampstead, and Junior U.K. Minister of Overseas Development. His books include *The Police; Participation and Poverty; Parks for People; The Foundations; The Police in Society* (1983); *A Bridge of People: A Personal View of Oxfam's First 40 Years* (1983); *Minorities: A Question of Human Rights* (1984); *The Global Connection: The Crisis of Drug Addiction* (1987); and *The Global Fix* (1988).

LIAH GREENFELD

John L. Loeb Associate Professor of Social Sciences, Harvard University, and Visiting Associate Professor in the Department of Political Science at the Massachusetts Institute of Technology, Liah Greenfeld has a Ph.D. from The Hebrew University in Jerusalem. In 1984 she was awarded a Mellon Fellowship. She was a John M. Olin Research Fellow from 1987 to 1988, and in 1989 and 1990 she was a member of the Institute for Advanced Studies in Princeton. Her books include *Different Worlds: A Study in the Sociology of Taste, Choice, and Success in Art* (1989), and *Center: Ideas and Institutions* (1988). Her *Nationalism: Five Roads to Modernity* was published in 1992 by Harvard University Press.

PETER M. OPPENHEIMER

Student of Christ Church, Oxford, Peter M. Oppenheimer received a B.A. in 1961 from The Queen's College, Oxford. He has been on the staff of the

Bank for International Settlements in Basle as a Research Fellow, and subsequently as Acting Investment Bursar, of Nuffield College, Oxford. From 1979 to 1989, he served on the council of the Trade Policy Research Centre, London, and he is currently on the Economic Advisory Panel and the Energy and Environment Panel of the Royal Institute for International Affairs. In 1976, he was Visiting Professor of International Finance at the London Business School. He also was a member of the Royal Commission on Legal Services from 1976 to 1979. In 1985 and 1986, he worked with Shell International as its Chief Economist. In 1991, he was a temporary economic attaché with the British Embassy in Moscow. A director of several companies, public and private, and a governor of four schools, he has also acted as consultant to international organizations and to business firms. He edited the book *Issues in International Economics* (1980).

KENNETH R. MINOGUE

Professor of Political Science at the London School of Economics and Political Science since 1984, Kenneth R. Minogue received a B.A. from Sydney University, and a B.Sc. in economics from the London School of Economics. He taught at the University of Exeter in 1955 and 1956. His publications include *The Liberal Mind* (1961), *Nationalism* (1967), *The Concept of a University* (1974), and *Alien Powers: The Pure Theory of Ideology* (1984). He has written widely both for academic journals and for journals such as *Encounter, The Times Literary Supplement, The National Interest,* and *The National Review.* He is a Member of the Thatcher Foundation and a Director of the Centre for Policy Studies.

ROGER SCRUTON

University Professor and Professor of Philosophy at Boston University, Roger Scruton received B.A., M.A., and Ph.D. degrees in philosophy from Jesus College, Cambridge, graduating with First Class Honors. He has been a lecturer at the University of Bordeaux; Research Fellow at Peterhouse, Cambridge; Director of Studies in Philosophy at Christ College, Cambridge; and Lecturer and Reader in Philosophy and Professor of Aesthetics at Birkbeck College at the University of London. He was a Visiting Professor for Architecture and Philosophy at Princeton University in 1979, a Visiting Professor at the University of Waterloo in 1980, a Distinguished Visiting Fellow at the University of Guelph in 1983, and a Scholar at the Hoover Institution for Peace and War in 1986. His books include *Art and Imagination* (1974), *The Meaning of Conservatism* (1980), *A Short History of Modern Philosophy* (1981), *The Politics of Culture* (1981), *Kant* (1982), *Sexual Desire* (1986), *The Philosopher on Dover Beach* (1991), and *Xanthippic Dialogues,* (1993). He founded, and has been editor of, *The Salisbury Review,* and is a founding member and trustee of the Jan Hus Educational Foundation and the Jagiellonian Trust, which helped to maintain the underground universities in Eastern Europe under the communist regimes.

JON WESTLING

Jon Westling was born in Yakima, Washington, and attended the public schools there. He was educated at Reed College, in Portland, Oregon, where he studied history and economics. Elected a Rhodes Scholar, he continued his work in history at Oxford University, and later at the University of California at Los Angeles. Mr. Westling taught at Centre College of Kentucky, Reed College, UCLA, and the University of California at Irvine before being recruited to Boston University by President John Silber in 1974. He served as Assistant to the President from 1976, and in 1979 was named Associate Provost. He was appointed Provost of Boston University in October 1984. During the 1987 sabbatical of President Silber, Mr. Westling served as Acting President of Boston University. In January 1988, he was named Executive Vice President for Administration and Academic Affairs. In 1990, when President Silber was on leave, Mr. Westling served as President *ad interim.*

PROGRAM OF THE CONVERSAZIONE

Each of the three participating universities in the *Boston, Melbourne, Oxford Conversazioni on Culture and Society* sponsors an international *conversazione* once every three years. On the occasion of its sesquicentennial celebration in 1989, Boston University inaugurated the series with "A Metaphor for Our Times." It was then Melbourne's turn, and in July 1990 La Trobe University was the host for the *conversazione* on "The Public Face of Architecture." In September 1991, Wadham College, Oxford, sponsored "Schools and Society" and in 1992 the *conversazione* returned to Boston University to consider "The Worth of Nations."

The Worth of Nations

NOVEMBER 12–14, 1992

BOSTON UNIVERSITY
THE TSAI PERFORMANCE CENTER
BOSTON, MASSACHUSETTS

THURSDAY, NOVEMBER 12

2 p.m.   Inaugural Session

The Worth of Nations

CHAIRMAN: Dr. John Silber
                             President of Boston University;
                             University Professor and Professor of
                             Philosophy and Law, Boston
                             University

Inaugural Address: Senator Daniel Patrick Moynihan
                             United States Senate

                             "Pandaemonium: Ethnicity in
                             International Politics"

9 a.m.   First Public Session

The Cultural Worth of Nations

CHAIRMAN:

Professor Roger Shattuck
University Professor and Professor of
Modern Foreign Languages and
Literatures, Boston University

Presentations by:

Professor Simon Schama
Professor of History, Harvard
University

"Woodland, Homeland,
Fatherland"

Professor Donald Carne-Ross
University Professor, William
Goodwin Aurelio Professor of
Greek Language and Literature,
Professor of Classics and Modern
Languages, Boston University

"Scott and the Matter of Scotland"

10:30 a.m. Respondents:

Professor Dame Leonie Kramer
Professor Emeritus of Australian
Literature and Chancellor of the
University of Sydney

Professor Benedict Anderson
Aaron L. Binenkorb Professor
of International Studies,
Cornell University

11 a.m.   Discussion

12 noon   Summing-up:

Professor Nathan Glazer
Professor of Education and Sociology,
Harvard University

FRIDAY, NOVEMBER 13

1:45 p.m.   Second Public Session

Empire and Aftermath

CHAIRMAN: Professor Brigitte Berger
                          Chairman, Department of Sociology,
                          Boston University

Presentations by: Hugh Trevor-Roper
                          Hon. Fellow and Former Master of
                          Peterhouse, Cambridge; Hon. Fellow of
                          Oriel College, Oxford

                          "The End of Empire in Europe"

                          Mr. Ben Whitaker
                          United Kingdom Member of the
                          United Nations Human Rights
                          Commission, 1975–88; Executive
                          Director, Minority Rights Group,
                          1971–88; Director, The Gulbenkian
                          Foundation, United Kingdom

                          "Ireland and Armenia: Lessons of
                          History?"

3:15 p.m.   Respondents: Professor Geoffrey Blainey
                          Professor Emeritus of History,
                          University of Melbourne

                          Mr. John O'Sullivan
                          Editor, The National Review

3:45 p.m.   Discussion

4:45 p.m.	Summing-up:	Professor Gertrude Himmelfarb *Professor Emeritus of History, City University of New York*
7 p.m.	Presentation by:	Mr. Bernard Levin *Chief Columnist,* The Times (London) " 'Thou Hast Multiplied the Nation, and Not Increased the Joy' — Isaiah 9.3"

SATURDAY, NOVEMBER 14

9:30 a.m.   Third Public Session

The Nation's Worth Transcended?

CHAIRMAN: Professor Uri Ra'anan
                         University Professor and Professor of
                         International Relations; Director,
                         Institute for the Study of Conflict,
                         Ideology, and Policy, Boston
                         University

Presentations by: Professor Liah Greenfeld
                         John L. Loeb Associate Professor of
                         Sociology, Department of Sociology,
                         Harvard University

                         "Transcending the Nation's
                         Worth"

                         Mr. Peter Oppenheimer
                         Student of Christ Church and
                         University Lecturer in Economics,
                         Oxford University

                         "Nationalism, Internationalism
                         and Economics"

11 a.m.   Respondents: Hugh Thomas
                         Historian, novelist, former Chairman
                         of the Centre for Policy Studies

                         Sir Arvi Parbo
                         Chairman, Western Mining
                         Corporation, Australia

11:30 a.m. Discussion

12:30 p.m. Summing-up: Ambassador Owen Harries
                         Editor, The National Interest

SATURDAY, NOVEMBER 14

2 p.m.   Fourth Public Session

            ## A New World of Nations

            CHAIRMAN: Professor Michael Osborne
                                     Professor Emeritus of Classics,
                                     University of Melbourne;
                                     Vice Chancellor, La Trobe
                                     University

            Presentations by: Professor Kenneth Minogue
                                     Professor of Political Science, London
                                     School of Economics and Political
                                     Science

                                     "Internationalism as an Emerging
                                     Ideology"

                                     Professor Roger Scruton
                                     University Professor and Professor of
                                     Philosophy, Boston University

                                     "The First Person Plural"

3:30 p.m.   Respondents: Professor Peter Berger
                                     University Professor and Professor of
                                     Sociology; Director, Institute for the
                                     Study of Economic Culture, Boston
                                     University

                                     Sr. Mario Vargas Llosa
                                     Robert F. Kennedy Visiting Professor
                                     of Latin American Studies,
                                     Harvard University

4 p.m.   Discussion

5 p.m.   Summing-up: Mr. Jon Westling
                                     Executive Vice President and Provost,
                                     Boston University

The Boston, Melbourne, Oxford
Conversazioni on Culture and Society

DATE DUE

DEMCO 38-296